Additional Praise for
Setting Profitable Prices

"You only need this workbook if you want to make more money."

—**William M. Turnoff**, CPA

"This workbook presents a fast way for entrepreneurs to set prices that will increase their chances for success. Entrepreneurs can't afford to leave money on the table, and the step-by-step models in this book will help prevent just that. Dr. Jensen runs a nano-incubator for new businesses at our Center. Now you can have her practical, easy-to-follow advice on pricing for your own new products or services."

—**Dr. Cori Myers**, Director, Haven Entrepreneurial Leadership Center

"This is great! Finally a practical user-friendly guide to pricing that I can use with my clients and students. The worksheets are valuable analytical tools that yield straightforward results that are easy to understand. We needed this!"

—**Mary Anne Holley**, Entrepreneurship Professor, Baruch College, CUNY

"I wish I had been able to use this workbook when I started my first business years ago. I'm sure I could have made more money! Reading this book is just as important as developing a sound business plan. I will definitely use her concepts in my courses on marketing."

—**Donna Coehelo**, Marketing Professor, WCSU

SETTING PROFITABLE PRICES

SETTING PROFITABLE PRICES

A Step-by-Step Guide to Pricing Strategy— Without Hiring a Consultant

Marlene Jensen

WILEY

John Wiley & Sons, Inc.

Published by John Wiley & Sons, Inc., Hoboken, New Jersey.
Published simultaneously in Canada.

For general information on our other products and services or for technical support, please contact our Customer Care Department within the United States at (800) 762–2974, outside the United States at (317) 572–3993, or fax (317) 572–4002.

Wiley publishes in a variety of print and electronic formats and by print-on-demand. Some material included with standard print versions of this book may not be included in e-books or in print-on-demand. If this book refers to media such as a CD or DVD that is not included in the version you purchased, you may download this material at booksupport.wiley.com. For more information about Wiley products, visit www.wiley.com.

Library of Congress Cataloging-in-Publication Data:

Jensen, Marlene.
    Setting profitable prices : a step-by-step guide to pricing strategy—without hiring a consultant/Marlene Jensen.
       p.   cm.
    Includes bibliographical references and index.
    ISBN 978-1-118-43076-7 (paper/website); 978-1-118-50266-2 (ebk); 978-1-118-50245-7 (ebk); 978-1-118-50273-0 (ebk)
       1. Pricing.   I. Title.
    HF5416.5.J46   2013
    658.8'16—dc23
                                                                                  2012037688

Printed in the United States of America.

10 9 8 7 6 5 4 3 2 1

This book is dedicated to my brother Harold Fann (1954–2008).

In 2005 we launched a two-person e-book company, where I did the marketing and he did the design (books and web sites).

Our first book—No-Cost Home Business Startup Plan—failed spectacularly, but when I switched to writing e-books about pricing and Harold wrote e-books about web site design, our company flourished.

After his surprise death from a heart attack, I learned how much of the enthusiasm and love I felt for the company was really enthusiasm for working with him and love for him. I still miss him terribly.

I thank him for getting me started writing about pricing—and for making it fun!

Contents

Preface

Setting *Profitable Prices* is a handbook that will guide you step-by-step to setting an optimal—profitable—price.

It is written for marketers, business owners, CFOs, and CEOs—anyone who needs to price a product or service. It is also for those who don't have the budget to hire a pricing consultant to advise them. A pricing consultant with a budget to do research for you will probably provide a more profitable price than you can yourself—even with this book. But a pricing consultant will cost anywhere from $10,000 up to hundreds of thousands of dollars. Plus $10,000 or more in research costs.

This handbook will walk you through steps a pricing consultant will use—steps you can take yourself to save the money. By following these steps, you should come up with a price that will produce far more profits than the average company without a pricing consultant. How do I know this? Because surveys show that most businesses use cost-plus pricing. In Chapter 2 you'll learn why this is a disaster for profitability. The next most used method is competitive pricing—another profit-killing method. Again, Chapter 2 will show you why.

This handbook will take you through the steps a pricing consultant will use in determining your optimal price. It won't include all of their steps—it won't do research for you!—but it will move you far closer to optimal than you can get without it.

Best of all, you get this profit advantage for the cost of a few hours of your time and the (ridiculously low!) price of this book.

Author Credentials

Who am I and why should you listen to my advice on pricing? Let me introduce myself.

I have a doctorate in marketing, with a dissertation on pricing new products. And I teach marketing and pricing, previously at New York University and Western Connecticut State University, currently at Lock Haven University.

Through my consulting company, Pricing Strategy Associates, I have consulted on pricing and new business development primarily for small companies, but also for AARP, Food Network, ABC, and *Playboy* magazine.

I am the author of the following books on pricing:

- *Pricing Psychology Report*
- *46 Ways to Raise Prices—Without Losing Sales*
- *The Tao of Pricing*

I have also done substantial research on pricing, which has been published in the following publications:

- **Journal of Product & Brand Management**
  - Translating country-of-origin effects into prices.
  - The changing price of brand loyalty under perceived time pressure.
  - Risk and acceptable maximum discount levels.
- **International Journal of Revenue Management**
  - Using consumer-perceived risks to set optimal discount levels.

- **International Journal of Business, Marketing, and Decision Sciences**
  - Can discounts be too deep? Consumer perceptions of product discounts during an economic downturn.
- **Proceedings of the Behavioral Pricing Conference**
  - Incumbent price responses to an entrant: a re-examination of previous research.
  - Risk factors that affect consumers' preferred discount levels.
  - Maximum acceptable discounts.
- **Proceedings of the International Academy of Business and Public Administration Disciplines**
  - Pricing of green products: premiums paid, consumer characteristics, and incentives.
  - Re-examining consumer acceptance of innovation.
- **Proceedings of the Northeast Business & Economics Association:**
  - Consumer processing of higher-than-expected prices.

If You Can Afford a Pricing Consultant . . .

If you have $40–$200K to spend on picking your best price(s), I recommend you hire a pricing consultant and insist on that person conducting discrete-choice conjoint pricing research for you.

You can find pricing consultants at PricingSociety.com (by clicking on their "Pricing Experts Directory"). Discrete-choice conjoint is the gold standard of pricing research, and one of the few methods of researching prices that produces reliable results—results you can safely use.

If you're talking to a pricing consultant who recommends research where you ask consumers the maximum they would expect to pay and the minimum they would expect to pay for your product, drop the consultant and get a better one. Results from this (and almost all other pricing "research") are completely unreliable in the real world. You want discrete choice research, perhaps with some other add-on research to answer sideline questions.

FYI, discrete choice research is *not* a do-it-yourself project. The software alone costs about $6,000, and the training to learn how to use it and analyze it would be another $3,000 or so, plus weeks and weeks of time. (Not to mention you'd need a couple of bottles of aspirin; my head hurt for weeks while I was learning it!)

Don't Have the Cash to Invest?

If you can't afford to hire a consultant, you're still in luck. Buying this book has cost you about the price of a good lunch. Using the techniques you'll get here could result in you getting the know-how *and* the research you need for no additional cost. At worst, you might need to spend an additional $200–$500 in research costs.

Can you sell your product or service online or through the mail—even if that will not be your primary method of sales? If your answer is "yes" then you are in luck. Using this book and concluding with online testing (as described in Chapters 11 and 12), should result in a very profitable price for your product or service. Maybe even close to what you could get using a consultant.

If you can't sell your product or service online or through the mail *and* you don't have the money for a consultant, then this book will help you price as profitably as you can without using those tools. But, know that using a price consultant would probably make a substantial difference for you.

How Big of a Rush Are You In?

This book contains 16 chapters and has four accompanying Excel worksheets that will guide you through setting the most profitable prices you can possibly set without hiring a pricing consultant and without conducting discrete choice pricing research.

If you can, read all the chapters and do all the Worksheets in detail.

However, as someone who ran businesses as a one-person operation, I know you often have to make time decisions that are less than optimal.

At the start of each chapter, and on the worksheets, I've indicated where you can cut corners—if you absolutely must. I also explain what you're risking by those shortcuts—so the choice is in your hands.

Chapter Summaries

Part 1: How to Set Prices for Maximum Profits is your introduction to profitable pricing.

- *Chapter 1: Why Pricing Is the Key to Your Success* will open your eyes about the profit impact of pricing decisions. Most businesspeople greatly underestimate the effect on profits of either raising or lowering prices.

- *Chapter 2: Why Most Companies Stink at Pricing (and How You Can Do Better!)* will show you the problems with the most common methods of setting prices. Surveys show that somewhere around 70–80 percent of all businesses use one of two pricing methods—both of which are likely to result in lower profits for you.

Part 2: How the Market Will Value Your New Product will help you determine how your customers will value your product/service.

- *Chapter 3: Analyzing Your Competitors' Prices* will show you how pricing consultants analyze your competition. Buyers typically look at prices relative to comparable product prices, so you need to get inside their heads to see how they will view your offerings.

  - **The Competitor Pricing Worksheet** will help you do this in a systematic manner. This worksheet can be found in the book's appendix, as well as on this book's companion web site.

- *Chapter 4: Environmental Factors That Can Affect Your Pricing* will walk you through outside influences that affect what consumers are willing to pay. These influences include economic conditions, technology changes, laws, regulatory changes, and cultural changes. Their effect on your pricing might be minimal—or it might be substantial.

- *Chapter 5: Pick the Positioning of Your New Product* will help you find the optimal position for your pricing. What does that mean? People will make many judgments about your product/service based on the price you pick. It sends out signals to consumers. For optimal pricing you need to be in charge of the signals you're sending! For example, pricing a new product with a low price will automatically cause consumers to worry about its quality. Do you want to be the cheap, quality-suspect brand? The high-quality brand? Or??

- *Chapter 6: Analyzing Your Buyer Benefits/Drawbacks Relative to Your Competitors* will help you view your offerings against your competitors by looking through their eyes. This will help you decide how much more (or how much less) than your competitors' prices buyers will expect from you. And, if the expectation is unfavorable, how to change it!

  - **The Buyer Benefits Worksheet** will help you do this in a systematic manner. This worksheet can be found in the book's appendix, as well as on this book's companion web site.

- *Chapter 7: Picking a "Ballpark" for Your Best Price* will start narrowing down your price choices. This starting point will already be better than most of your competitors, based as it will be upon the content already covered—competitor prices, value differences between your product/service and theirs, your product positioning, and current environmental factors. Once you have this range, the remainder of the book will help you narrow it to your most profitable price.

  - **The Narrowing Your Price Range Worksheet** will help you do this in a systematic manner. This worksheet can be found in the book's appendix, as well as on this book's companion web site.

Part 3: Your Cost Analysis will help you determine your costs.

- *Chapter 8: Evaluating Your Costs*—a "reality check"—will help you look at your costs to get a floor for your pricing. It will help you calculate your total costs—including fixed and variable costs—and evaluate what your profits would be giving the price range you selected in Chapter 7.

  - **The Cost Analysis Worksheet** will help you do this in a systematic manner. This worksheet can be found in the book's appendix, as well as on this book's companion web site.

Part 4: Fine-Tuning Your Price will help you insure your price will be optimal for profits.

- *Chapter 9: Is Your Profit Potential Acceptable?* helps you save the day if your target price won't deliver enough profits. After looking at the price range you developed and your costs, many businesses will find the profit potential isn't there or isn't enough. Or you may just be hoping for more. This chapter gives you multiple options to add profits to your offering. Note: This chapter alone pays you back for this book. Why settle for less profit?

- *Chapter 10: Psychological Adjustments to Your Price* shows you how to make tiny adjustments (pennies or a dollar or two) to your prices that can result in large increases in units sold.

Part 5: Testing Your Prices will help you test your prices.

- *Chapter 11: Testing Prices* will show you why you need to test prices and help you evaluate the best methods of testing for your product or service. It will show you the difference between research and testing, and help you pick the cheapest, *reliable* method for testing.

- *Chapter 12: Using Google to Test for Free (or Almost Free)* will give you the specifics you need to set up an AdWords test or a Google Optimizer test. It will walk you through the steps needed to set up an A/B split test (where you test two or three different prices for exactly the same product). It will also show you how you can combine price tests with headline and other tests—to get the maximum amount of feedback in the shortest period of time.

Part 6: Pricing in Special Situations will provide additional pricing help for specific pricing situations.

- *Chapter 13: Pricing Services* provides additional help when you're pricing a service instead of a product. Pricing services carries a number of differences and complications we typically don't see in pricing products.

- *Chapter 14: Pricing New Products/Services, Part 1: When Your Brand Is Unknown* gives you insights from all the pricing research focused on brands unknown to consumers.

- *Chapter 15: Pricing New Products/Services, Part 2: Competing with Established Brands* looks at research that shows how much of a price premium established brands can possess, and at the various different price positions that will give you the maximum profit opportunities when you compete against known brands.

- *Chapter 16: Pricing with Discounts* provides you with the latest research on what works best and what doesn't in discounting. It also points out where research has uncovered dangers in discounting to future profits. The chapter concludes with some final thoughts on taking this new expertise with you, with confidence, into future pricing situations. While you probably bought this book for a one-time problem, it will help you for the rest of your career! It can be the framework of how you approach each new pricing situation—to earn the most for yourself and your company.

Acknowledgments

Thanks go to Dr. Ron Drozdenko for pulling me into academic research when I was only an adjunct professor, and for showing me how to do better research and better analysis. And for being willing to let me run with all the pricing research that interested me instead of other topics.

Thanks also to our co-researcher Donna Coelho for her skill and support.

Thanks to Dr. Calvin Berkey at Argosy University, whose mentorship helped convince me I could handle—and would enjoy—all the work involved in going for a doctorate.

Thanks to the business and computer science faculty at Lock Haven University for creating a welcoming and challenging environment where I could continue to learn, research, teach, consult, and publish.

Thanks to the editors at Wiley who turned out to be extremely supportive, collaborative, and skilled (unlike my experiences at a different publisher!). Special thanks to my editor, Debra Englander; development editor, Tula Batanchiev; copyeditor Jodi Brandon; and senior production editor, Stacey Fischkelta, who together this book far better than I could have done alone.

Finally, thanks to my agent, Agnes Birnbaum of Bleeker Street Associates, for her skill and knowledge that placed this book with the right publisher for its success. And for decades of her sterling advice and friendship.

PART 1

How to Set Prices for Maximum Profits

In the first chapters, you'll learn:

- Just how much money you can make—or lose!—from your pricing decisions.
- Why most companies stink at it.

The biggest pricing problem for small to medium-sized companies is that you don't often have extra time and a consulting budget to make the best pricing decisions. If researching the best price means weeks of work, a migraine headache, and a desire to slit your wrists rather than read even one more demand chart, then you're more likely to join your competitors in making pricing mistakes. You'll see those problems in Chapter 2.

But, now you don't have to make their mistakes. You've got this book and its worksheets (found in the appendix and online at this book's companion web site).

Setting Profitable Prices is a very practical book, because my interest in pricing is practical. Yes, I'm an academic who teaches pricing and marketing at a university. But that's a new career for me. I've previously spent decades marketing for large and small companies, and decades as an entrepreneur. I'm only interested in pricing theory if it provably *works*.

CHAPTER 1

Why Pricing Is the Key to Your Success

Of all the marketing problems you face in launching a new product, pricing is the most important—and the most difficult!

Want proof?

If your new product costs you, say, $45 to produce, and you sell it for $69, your profit—what you can take home with you—is $24.

- If you price that same product $10 higher, you get to pocket the entire $10 extra—resulting in $34 profit instead of $24.

- If you price your product $10 lower, you lose out of your pocket the full $10—resulting in $14 profit instead of $24.

If you sell more of your products, the profit is reduced by your costs of making the extra products. For example, you get an extra sale that brings in $45, but only $24 of that is actual profit.

Raise Prices—or Sell More Products?

Ask most businesspeople what they could do to dramatically increase their profits, and their answers are usually:

- Increase my advertising
- Add more salespeople
- Add incentives to buy more

All three strategies would probably sell more products, but they are risky. The first two will increase your costs—for which you *hope* to then get a payoff in increased sales and (hopefully) profits. The third strategy will lower your profit margin, so you're earning less per unit sold.

Yet these three answers miss the most obvious way to dramatically increase profits: a price raise.

Let's analyze what is best for profits—10 percent more sales (units) or a 10 percent higher price.

If you are currently selling $100,000 worth of a product, take a look at Exhibit 1.1 to see what would happen.

Only with pricing does everything—plus or minus— fall to the bottom line.

You may object to Exhibit 1.1. You might figure that if you raise prices you will sell fewer products. That happens often, but not always.

So let's look at the same situation—if your units sold were to drop 10 percent when you raise prices 10 percent. Now it would look like Exhibit 1.2.

Note that in Exhibit 1.2, you'd have:

- $2,500 more profits—selling 10 percent more units
- $10,000 more profits—with a 10 percent higher price
- $6,500 more profits—with a 10 percent higher price even if it lowered units sold by 10 percent

What has that meant for companies? What could it mean for you? Typically, with the cost structure at most companies, a 1 percent increase in price yields a 12 percent gain in profits (Dolan and Simon, 1996).

There's simply no marketing decision you can make with as strong an impact on your profits as pricing.

EXHIBIT 1.1 PRICE EFFECT ON PROFITS

Change	Revenues	Costs	Profits
Base Case	$100,000	75,000	$25,000
10% more units sold	$10,000 increase	$7,500 increase	$2,500 increase
10% higher price	$10,000 increase	No increase	$10,000 increase

EXHIBIT 1.2 PRICE EFFECT ON PROFITS

Change	Units	Price	Revenues	Costs	Profits
Base Case	10,000	$10	$100,000	75,000	$25,000
10% more units sold	1,000 increase	No change	$10,000 increase	$7,500 increase	$2,500 increase
10% higher price	No increase	$1 increase	$10,000 increase	No increase	$10,000 increase
10% higher price AND 10% fewer units sold	1,000 DECREASE	$1 increase	$1,000 DECREASE	$7,500 DECREASE	$6,500 increase

Big-Company Case History

When Volkswagen launched the [new Beetle] in the United States, orders flooded in, quickly resulting in consumers waiting nine months for a car. The value customers placed on owning a new Beetle, coupled with the nostalgic effect, was clearly underestimated, and one could make the assumption that a $500 or $1,000 higher price might not have affected sales dramatically but would have significantly increased profits.

Butscher and Laker, 2000

Can you imagine the impact an extra $1,000 in the U.S. price would have had for Volkswagen (VW)? They sold 83,000 new Beetles in the U.S. in 1999. That means whoever picked the price for it may have lost Volkswagen $83 million in profits. Not just in sales—but in profits. And this only counts the first year, not subsequent years.

Yet in Germany, VW had the opposite problem. Their sales were poor due to a "steep" price that Butscher and Laker say overestimated the value Germans put on the car.

Another example is the launch of the Wii. Demand was so strong for the product that stores had waiting lists to get one. An extra $50 on the price wouldn't have harmed sales at all. Instead consumers lucky enough to buy a Wii were able to resell immediately at a profit of $100 or $125 over the company's price. So profits that could have (should have?) gone to Wii, went instead to scalpers!

Be sure *you* don't throw away money like this!

Tiny-Company Case History

When I launched my first newsletter (*Ancillary Profits*) I wasn't very smart about pricing. I knew that $100 was perceived as much bigger than $99 and I came out of the magazine publishing industry, not newsletters. In the magazine industry $20 was a big price. So I priced *Ancillary Profits* at $97—without even testing other prices.

Fortunately, I decided three months later to test higher prices. In addition to $97, I tested $117 and $127. The winner was $127. It not only gave me $30 more per subscription, but it even brought in 11 percent *more orders*. That means I was able to pocket 45 percent more profits from just a $30 price increase.

And I was still being stupid. The highest price I tested won. I should have tested even higher. When I did, I was able to get more profits from a $147 price! (Later, even more from $197.)

I calculated how much I lost from not starting at the higher price—and found I'd lost about $38,000 in *profits*. And if I hadn't done the three tests within 12 months, it would have been much, much more. Moral of the story: Always test a price that is much higher than you think you can get.

Hopefully, you're now convinced at how important pricing is to your bottom line.

The problem is that good pricing can be difficult. So difficult that most smaller companies just throw up their hands and take one of two "easy" ways out (both of which can cost you a lot of money!):

- Cost-plus pricing
- Match-your-competitors pricing

We'll cover cost-plus and match-your-competitors pricing strategies in the next chapter.

CHAPTER 2

Why Most Companies Stink at Pricing (and How You Can Do Better!)

Pricing is a specialty topic in marketing—one with very few practitioners. You can get a doctorate in marketing (like I did) without ever taking a course on pricing. That's because most marketing professors don't know enough about the topic to be teaching it. There's an annual pricing conference for academics and there are typically only 30 to 40 of us there each year—and that includes a number of professors from outside the United States.

Most people with specialized pricing skills are working in or have their own pricing consultancy. You can find me and the other pricing consultants at PricingSociety .com under their Pricing Experts Directory. Other pricing specialists work at very large companies and multinationals that can afford their own in-house pricing staff.

If you're a new, small, or medium-sized company, this means there's nobody who can give you the pricing help you need. Not unless you've got an extra $30–$250K you can afford for a consultant.

What can you do on your own? You can buy a book on pricing and hope to learn what you need from it. The best all-around book on pricing strategy is *The Strategy and Tactics of Pricing* by Nagle, Holden, and Zale. If you can take the time, I recommend it. I even use it when I teach pricing. However, it can be pretty rough going for a newbie. I was already a pricing specialist when I first read it, and it still took weeks of my time and most of my focus to process it. And it has an academic focus—which means it doesn't give any of the quick answers business owners and marketers need.

Also, ask yourself what your goal is. Do you want to learn to become a pricing specialist? Or do you just want to price your products for maximum profit and then move on to the million other decisions you need to make?

Buying *this* book is a smart alternative. It won't give you the all-around knowledge you'll get from Nagle and Holden's book. However, it will get you through your pricing decision in a day (if that's all you have) or a week (if you can spare more time for a better decision). And it will leave you with a much better—more profitable—price than your competitors.

The "Myth" of Creating Demand Curves

One of the biggest headaches you'll get from a textbook on pricing—and also in blogs and articles on pricing that are, in my opinion, worthless—is they will tell you to create demand curves to capture the price elasticity of demand.

In normal English, that means you are to track how many units you can sell at different prices—so you can find the most optimal price. Well, duh! If you already know that you can sell 6.5 percent more units at price "A" and 4.3 percent more at price "B," then your decision is easy. You just calculate the profits and total sales at each price and your decision is made for you.

Just one teeny problem with this: It's worthless advice for almost everyone. You'd first need to:

- Offer your product or service at 15–20 different prices to see how many sell.

- Offer each different price for long enough to get at least 40 sales for each price (so the results gain some statistical reliability).

- Offer all 15–20 different prices at the same time (otherwise your results could be skewed by a time variable).

- Keep people from finding out about all these different prices—or they'll skew the test results (hard to do especially with services).

Because you'll not be able to do all the above, and will therefore cut corners trying, the data you come up with will likely be wrong. That means no matter how impressive your demand curve charts look, making pricing decisions on them would be ill advised.

Businesses that have been selling the same product for ages at lots of different prices might be able to create demand curves. But they would be comparing sales at price "A" six months ago versus sales at price "B" three months ago. I wouldn't trust there's been no change in product demand for price "A" in six months, and you shouldn't either.

Forget demand curves! With this book you won't need them.

How Your Competitors Are Setting Prices

There is some question as to whether cost-plus pricing or competitive pricing is the most prevalent.

Nagle and Holden (2002) say **cost-plus pricing** is the most prevalent. This strategy adds up your costs then tacks on an extra percentage of the total for profits. Use of this (generally terrible) strategy is often the result of the pricing decision being left to the finance department or to an entrepreneur who doesn't understand pricing.

Noble and Gruca (1999) found **competitive pricing** was used by three times as many companies they studied as any other strategy. They define competitive pricing as trying to match or come in close to the prices of the competing products already on the market.

If you had to pick one of the two above, pick the second one. Match-your-competitors pricing will lose you less than cost-plus.

But why use either?

If your competitors are small to medium-sized companies, they're likely using one of these false strategies already. So you can gain a substantial advantage over them by using better strategies. If your competitors are large companies, well, you're already at a disadvantage. You don't want to increase it!

Cost-Plus Pricing

What is cost-plus pricing? It is a price that includes your costs plus a fixed percentage (15 percent or 50 percent—whatever your target is) for profits. Example: You need to price a new product that costs you $85 for materials. You estimate it also needs to cover $15 of your overhead. So your total costs are $100. You want to make 15 percent profit, so you price this product at $115.

Sounds great, right? You cover your costs. You get a guaranteed 15 percent profit. What could be better?

Actually, almost any other pricing strategy is better. Cost-plus pricing should be used *only* when you sell custom products. If you build custom houses, then you need to use cost-plus pricing. Using this strategy for any other situation is throwing away money.

Two Ways This Strategy Can Make You *Lose* Money

The "guaranteed" profit from cost-plus pricing can actually lose you money. You could be throwing away profits, or you could actually end up selling your products for lower than your costs! Here are the deadly duo of ways this strategy will hurt you:

1. Because your "variable costs" really do vary

Variable costs are just that: variable. They depend on how many you buy. In the previous example, your $85 for materials depends on the quantity you order of each. Let's say you projected you would sell 500 products every month. So you order 1,000 (two months' worth) of materials for those products at a time for a total cost of $85 each. What happens if you find you can only sell 250 each month? The next time you order for two months, you'll only order 500. So the vendors will charge you a higher price. Your actual price might come out to $100 each instead of $85. With your $15 of overhead, your actual costs are $115 instead of $100.

■ In this example, you set your price to get a "guaranteed" profit of 15 percent. You thought your costs would be $100, giving you $15 profit for each item you sell. But since you're only selling half as many as you thought you would, your costs are $115—so you're receiving *zero* dollars of profit for each item.

■ What happened to your "guaranteed" profits? Gone. In fact, you could even end up *losing* money on each item you sell with this pricing strategy.

■ If this is a *new* product you're offering, you really can't know how many you will sell. You can do the best marketing research in the world and still be terribly off in the number of units you sell. Think of the Wii introduction—where backorders went on for months! They did extensive research on demand, only to be terribly wrong. Think of Segway—which thought hundreds of thousands of us would be scooting around town on their machines. Since you really can't know what demand will be, cost-plus pricing will *not* give you the "guaranteed" profits you expect.

2. Because you haven't accounted for consumer perceptions of value

Suppose you guessed right about the quantity you would sell. So you got your planned 15 percent ($15) profit on each item. That's great, right? Should you be celebrating? Not necessarily! You might just have cost yourself thousands and thousands of dollars.

How? What if the people who wanted this product and bought it at $115, would have been just as willing to pay $130? You could have had *double* the profits you're actually getting for each item. You just cost yourself—or your company—a lot of money. And you will continue to lose that money until the day you learn how to set a better price.

Match-Your-Competitors Pricing

Planning to match your competitors' prices is recommended only in two, frankly unlikely, sets of circumstances:

1. When your new product is almost identical to the competitor products already being sold

2. When your new product has very little advantage over competitor products *and* the competitors are pretty tame (e.g., when they don't compete hard against each other)

Why are they unlikely?

1. Why the heck would anyone launch a product that's not different or has little to no competitive advantage? Most people stick to a brand that works for them. To get them to try a different one requires a reason. "Me-too" products don't provide a reason.

2. Very, very few markets have competitors who don't compete. Most markets have competitors who are watching every penny change made by a competitor.

This is not to say you ignore competitor prices. Not at all! They are a wonderful source of free research for you. Reviewing your competitors' prices tells you what your target customers are willing to pay for products with some similarities to yours. You don't have to guess they're willing to pay those prices. Your competitors' sales prove it!

The problem with pricing a new product relative to your competitors is that it doesn't give you enough price "bonus" for your product's advantages over the competitors. It also doesn't account well for any negatives your product has relative to the competitors.

For example, suppose you create a new product that is 10 percent better than the competitors. What is that extra 10 percent of effectiveness worth to consumers? Maybe not a single penny more. Or maybe double or triple your competitors' prices.

Want proof? Here are two examples:

1. Suppose you make soap. You discover something you can add to your soap that will make it clean 10 percent better. And you can prove it. The process will cost you an extra 10 percent in costs, so you want to get at least 10 percent more in price. Can you get it?

    Ask yourself if you would be willing to pay 10 percent more for soap that is proven to clean 10 percent better. Most people wouldn't. They feel the soap they're using cleans well enough.

2. Now suppose, instead, you make anti-wrinkle creams. And you've discovered an ingredient that will reduce the

appearance of wrinkles by 10 percent. But the ingredient will add 10 percent to your wrinkle cream costs.

Can you get 10 percent more in price for a 10 percent better wrinkle cream? We both know you can probably get 100 percent more in price for it. Maybe even 200 percent more.

The *value* of your new product has no basis in your costs or the degree of improvement over competitor products. The value to your customers is in the degree to which they *want* your new advantage.

Matching your competitors' prices doesn't capture the true value to consumers of your product's specific benefits. Nor does it recognize your product's disadvantages compared to competitors.

Both of these can cause the *value* of your product or service to differ substantially from your competitors. So matching competitor prices could lose you the price premium you could have commanded (because you are underpriced for the value you deliver) and/or lose you substantial unit sales because you're overpriced for your perceived value.

PART 2

How the Market Will Value Your New Product

As marketers or entrepreneurs, we get so caught up in our products/services that it's hard to evaluate them from the potential buyer's perspective. We're either in love with them, or we convince ourselves we are so that we can better market them.

I can't tell you how often in management meetings at ABC and then at CBS I listened to executives discount competitor's products/services as inferior to ours. Fortunately for me, I was able to see through the blindness because I was first at ABC where their executives were certain their *High Fidelity* and *Modern Photography* magazines were clearly superior, followed by a management position at CBS where their executives were equally convinced that *their* magazines—*Audio* and *American Photographer*—were superior. Both sets of executives clearly could not be right.

The same applies to individual perceptions. If you ask businesspeople to rank their abilities compared to their peers, more than 85 percent will rank themselves in the top 50 percent. And they are sincere in their beliefs! But the math just doesn't work.

In some ways it's similar to parents who can't see all the faults of their children, or who see them as minor problems when they're really major problems. We love our babies, our projects, our businesses.

This blindness is why there are five chapters in this section. They're designed to remove the blinders we all develop, and look clearly and unemotionally through the eyes of your potential buyers.

- How do *they* see your product/service?
- How do *they* see the offerings of your competitors?
- What do *they* value in your type of product/service?
- How will *they* feel if they pay a lower price? A higher price?
- Do *they* perceive a prestige factor in this type of product/service? If not, would they like to?
- Are *they* sensitized to prices right now due to economic conditions?
- What do *they* think is a fair price for your product/service? What do they perceive as being unfair?

These five chapters will show you:

- How to investigate your competitors—through the eyes of your buyers.
- Environmental factors that will affect the price you can command.
- The science of price positioning—how to know what your price is saying about your products and how to change it if needed. Also included here are materials designed to prevent price positioning mistakes and keep you out of price wars.
- How to analyze your product/service versus your competitors—again through the buyers' eyes.
- Where to start when picking a price range.

Learn More

Buyers who perceive a price or pricing strategy as unfair will often pay a higher price or otherwise economically harm themselves in order to extract revenge—to punish the company with "unfair" prices.

More on this interesting phenomenon can be seen in an excellent book titled *The Price Is Wrong: Understanding What Makes a Price Seem Fair and the True Cost of Unfair Pricing* by Sarah Maxwell.

CHAPTER 3

Analyzing Your Competitors' Prices

In-a-Rush Tip

Do *not* skip this critical chapter or the worksheet for it. But if you are in a rush, you *can* narrow your focus to your three or four primary competitors and your primary products.

Warning: By limiting yourself to fewer competitors, you will miss out on uncovering some add-on opportunities for extra profits for your product/service.

Before you ever launch your new product, consumers have expectations about what your price *should* be. Those expectations come from what your competitors charge for their products. You need to know those expectations.

You *Do So* Have Competitors!

I'm always surprised at the number of entrepreneurs who believe their product is so different they don't have competitors. Every product sold today has competitors.

Proof that everyone has competitors:

The marketers who launched the Segway motorized scooter a few years back probably had more reason than most to believe they didn't have competitors. But they did. Their competitors are anything anyone buys that will make going short distances easier and faster.

Segway competitors listed in order of price consumers pay:

- Skateboard
- Rollerblades

- Bike

- Motorbike

- Motorcycle

- Golf cart for in-town use

- Car

How to "Pick" Your Competitors

Sometimes you can get customers to accept a higher price for your product by "picking" your competitors.

For example, business newsletters had a pricing problem. To be profitable, they need to price themselves somewhere between $300 and $1,500. But their customers are used to paying $39–$75 for *Fortune, Forbes,* or *Business Week.* Even the daily *Wall Street Journal* can be had (in print!) for $155/year. So business newsletter marketers learned to compare a business newsletter to a different category—consulting expenses (e.g., "You can spend just $475/year on XYZ newsletter and stay on top of hazardous waste regulations—*or* you can spend $15,000/year for a consultant!").

So they've painted their competitive landscape (in order of price) as shown in Exhibit 3.1.

In this situation, newsletter publishers can either compare their products to the *Wall Street Journal*—and look overpriced—or compare their products to consultants and look like a great bargain!

Direct vs. Indirect Competitors

Direct competitors are those products consumers are most likely to substitute for your product as an alternative. Consider them "equivalent" products.

Your direct competitors are also likely to be where consumers get their ideas as to what a "fair" price would be for your product. See Exhibit 3.2.

It gets a little more complicated if you don't have a competitor as close as in Exhibit 3.2. Then your "direct" competitors may be a little broader group, such as shown in Exhibit 3.3.

Indirect competitors are less directly competitive with you. They are items consumers *could* substitute for your

EXHIBIT 3.1 CHOOSING YOUR COMPETITORS

Business Magazines ➡ *Wall Street Journal* ➡ Business Newsletters ➡ Consultants

EXHIBIT 3.2 DIRECT COMPETITORS	
Your Product	**Your DIRECT Competitor(s)**
Toxic Waste Today **(newsletter)**	*Toxic Waste Review* (newsletter)
Online research service	SurveyMonkey.com and Zoomerang.com
Grocery store	Any grocery within 3–4 miles of yours
Freelance writer on family topics	Any other freelance writer on family topics

EXHIBIT 3.3 LESS DIRECT COMPETITORS	
Your Product	**Your DIRECT Competitor(s)**
The only toxic waste newsletter	Toxic waste magazines
The only grocery store in town	Any local convenience store (including marts at gas stations)
Freelance writer on family topics	Freelance writers on home or personal topics

EXHIBIT 3.4 INDIRECT COMPETITORS	
Your Product	**Your INDIRECT Competitor(s)**
Segway	Golf carts, motor scooters, bikes, and rollerblades
The only grocery store in town	Restaurants, fast food places
Athletic shoes	Dress shoes, sandals
Beer	Wine, hard liquor

product, but that they probably would *not*. For example, if you sell hiking boots, consumers *could* buy dress shoes instead—but they probably would not. But dress shoes will protect your feet, just like hiking boots will.

If you are about to launch a product as unique as Segway was, then you really don't have direct competitors. You have only indirect competitors. Exhibit 3.4 offers a few examples.

For example, look at the problems Segway faced. They got great publicity by having news media people try out a Segway. They showed up on the news, on morning shows, in magazines; they got millions (maybe billions!) of dollars

Warning

It is *not* a good thing if you have no direct competitors—only indirect. It will probably force you to do "missionary" marketing, which is the most difficult marketing of all.

of free advertising. But consumers, for the most part, didn't buy. Instead, Segways today are purchased mainly by security personnel at shopping centers and universities, and police in congested big cities.

If people aren't already buying a product that would be a direct competitor, then you have to convince people they need a product they have never thought they needed. For example, when Apple launched the iPod, they didn't have to do missionary marketing. People were already used to buying things (portable radios and tape decks) that would let them take their music with them. The iPod just made it easier.

How Consumers Evaluate Prices

While many consumers do know the going price of staple products (bread, milk, and a few other items they buy frequently), most consumers have no idea what your price is or was.

Research by de Chernatony and Knox (1992) found just 15 percent of shoppers remembered the price of Evian bottled water and 6 percent the price of Del Monte fruit juice. Just 59 percent were able to give the price within a plus or minus 15 percent range. They conclude that consumer behavior is based on relative price assessments, not on absolute numbers.

A "reference price" is a price in the mind of consumers as to what they would expect to pay for your kind of product.

- In a few staple product cases, it's an actual price.

- More often it's a general range (e.g., "low $30" or "$400 something").

- Frequently consumers have no particular price number in mind when they start considering a purchase; they develop their reference price when they start looking

Exception

In a business-to-business market, buyers can simply look up your last price—and are buying in a quantity to merit that expenditure of their time.

at the competitor options. This is almost always true with products or services consumers buy infrequently.

So, let's picture the scenario. A consumer decides he or she might want to purchase your kind of product or service. The consumer starts looking at the choices available and finds:

- Choice A, a high-quality brand, for $28
- Choice B, a recognized brand, for $25
- Choice C, an unknown brand, for $24
- Choice D, a recognized brand, for $22
- Choice E, an unknown brand, for $21

What does the consumer now perceive/believe based on this "research" (which could just be looking at choices on a grocery shelf)? He or she now believes:

- The price for this product or service should be in the $20s. *(This becomes the reference price.)*
- The consumer can treat him- or herself to the best quality for just $3–$4 extra *(if the consumer decides it's worth it).*
- Choice E is a poor-quality product *(even though it might be acceptable).*
- Choice C becomes invisible (unless *it has some differentiation that is appealing to the consumer).*

Additional pricing knowledge you can gain from this scenario: If you want to charge more than $28, you'd better have a compelling, easy-to-grasp advantage—that matters to consumers—over your competitors.

While a new product can enter the market outside the price range of competitive products, it must be positioned in such a way as to explain the reasoning to customers. Specifically, it must address quality fears if it is below the range and it must stress additional benefits if it is above the range (Nagle and Holden, 2002).

How to Get Profitable Ideas from Your Competitors

To take this first critical step in setting your prices, go to Chapter 3's Competitor Pricing Worksheet in the Appendix. Look at the tabs at the bottom to find the type of business closest to yours. Your choices are:

- Service Business
- Product Business
- Sponsor Opportunities

What do you get out of filling in the details for more than your closest two or three competitors? Maybe opportunities to add a lot more profits to your bottom line!

Notice that under "service" or "offering," there are more lines for "add-ons." The more competitors you investigate, the more add-ons you will uncover. Some of them may not be right for you, but others may be worth thousands (or millions!) of dollars to you over time.

If your competitors have had a price war and are keeping the basic cost of their product/service at a really low price, you may find they make *all* or almost all their profits from the add-ons.

You'll need it later in the book to determine to your best—most profitable—price(s).

Your Assignment

Fill out the Competitor Pricing Worksheet today!

CHAPTER 4

Environmental Factors That Can Affect Your Pricing

In-a-Rush Tip

Read under the headings "The Economy" and "Competitors," but you can skip the rest of the chapter. However, skim the headlines to make sure you aren't skipping a critical area for your industry.

Environmental Factors Overview

Environmental factors that marketers consider in setting prices are factors that are beyond the control of the company. They include:

- The economy
- Competitors
- Government regulation and legal

- Social trends
- Technological change

The Economy

The economy can have a large influence on the optimal price for your new product. But, it won't affect all prices, so a knee-jerk lower price in a bad economy isn't your smartest move. Following are some observations based on my years in pricing products and services:

- Don't be the first competitor to lower prices in a bad economy. Here's why:
  - Your customers won't feel any extra loyalty to you for it; in bad economies, consumers think lower prices are just what they deserve. They absolutely will not love you for it—or even thank you for it.
  - Your competitors will probably then lower theirs, resulting in lower prices becoming etched in stone.
  - Maybe if you don't lower prices, neither will your competitors. Then you'll have a healthier profit margin in bad times.
- If your product is a necessity, you are less likely to need to discount.
- If you sell to consumers, you are more likely to need to discount—starting with the most expensive items such as cars and major appliances.
- If the bad economy drags on (as it did in 2010–2011), some consumers will discount shop even for the least expensive items. However, this doesn't mean consumers won't splurge. A premium bubble bath should always have a solid market, as long as it is marketed as a "little luxury" to relieve stress.
- When consumers give up big things (such as vacations, new appliances, etc.), they want to treat themselves to smaller luxuries.
- Selling to businesses in a bad economy sometimes seems to require ESP. As the economy worsens, businesses typically still spend on anything that advances the business. Until suddenly they don't.
  - Businesses typically start cutting advertising and sponsorship money about three months into a recession. (And they lag three months into a recovery before they increase it.) Media typically start discounting when the cutbacks come.
  - Once a purchasing agent becomes involved in the buying decision, it's a signal that some amount of discounting will be required, especially if the agent wasn't previously part of the process.

Be careful in a recovery about raising prices. Consumers have strong gut reactions to what they perceive as "fair" in pricing. This is despite our capitalist definition of fair prices—that a fair price is what a willing buyer is willing to pay and a willing seller is willing to accept. That definition doesn't always hold when prices go up.

Launching a new product with a higher price isn't likely to run into the "fairness" problem, but raising the price on something already offered might. Particularly vulnerable to consumer wrath are:

- Necessities, such as food and rent.

- Disaster needs. After a hurricane tears down houses, a lumber yard might be able to get a very large price increase due to heavy demand. But they are risking a public relations disaster.

- Anything where consumers can find out someone else got a better price. In a fascinating book I highly recommend, *The Price is Wrong* by Sarah Maxwell, the author has research to show that what turns ordinary price grumbling into ballistic antagonism is less about the price itself than about two things:

  - Is the company fattening its pockets at the expense of desperate people? (see "Disaster needs" mentioned previously), or

  - Is somebody else getting a better price than they can get?

In times of economic change, you need to watch and understand your customers even more than usual. If price is secondary to other features (speed of delivery? warrantee?) then use restraint in lowering a price. But also watch your competitors. If a key competitor lowers its price, you will need to move quickly *if* you find it's hurting your sales. But don't assume it will. Make sure. Also, by watching your competitors closely in an upturn, you may be able to more easily raise your prices when a competitor does so first.

Warnings:

1. It is illegal to talk to your competitors about prices. But it is not illegal to watch their actions and respond where appropriate.

2. Think hard before matching a price cut. They often lead to price wars and a permanently lower price your type of product/service can command. Try to find something else—*anything* else—you can use to differentiate yourself and your products/services.

   - A desired feature competitors don't have makes people willing to pay you a premium.

   - Offering faster turnaround and payment over time are methods of competing successfully against a lower price.

3. If a competitor raises prices, raise yours quickly if your product is comparable. The extra units you might sell from not raising your price seldom produce enough profits to make up for the higher price you could have commanded.

4. If you're the leader in a market, and you want to raise prices, you can raise your prices then see if your competitors follow suit. If they don't, you can legally lower your prices back. You might then try again to raise them and see if your competitors follow suit. If your competitors are smart, they will raise theirs as well.

Competitors

The financial strength, number, and pricing-savvy of your competitors will all affect the price you can charge.

Stupid competitors can lower profits for all companies, sometimes even making an entire industry unprofitable. My definition of stupid competitors includes the following:

- Those who will always cut price to make a sale. They often find themselves in price wars that nobody wins.
  - Examples:
    - ◆ Magazine printers cut margins again and again to steal business from each other until there wasn't enough profit to support any but the most efficient and most profitable printers. Many others went bankrupt.
    - ◆ The airline industry. Enough said!

- Those so addicted to the sales boost that they run constant sales, causing consumers to devalue the "fair" price for that type of product or service.
- Those who see the industry leader raising prices and don't at least consider jumping on the bandwagon.

On the other hand, if you're entering a field with one or more very powerful competitors, who keep prices low to discourage competition, you will have to differentiate yourself substantially in order to get buyers at an acceptably profitable price.

The good news is that by utilizing the Competitor Pricing Worksheet included in this book's Appendix, you'll be taking account of your competitive situation when you determine your optimal price(s).

Government Regulation and Legal

If the government regulates the prices you can charge, that is outside the scope of this book. Your "pricing" department is more a lobbying department.

But non-price government regulations can also affect your prices. Government regulations can change your product from "nice to have" to "required to have."

As an example, consider new regulations about protecting the safety of your customer data, such as social security numbers, credit card numbers, etc. Companies that had spent as little as possible to do a "so-so" job, must now spend more—or face big financial penalties in addition to very bad press. In fact, the only price-limiting factor when government regulations turn your product/service into a requirement will be the number of new competitors that will jump into the market—many with lower prices.

Governments have a number of specific pricing regulations that companies need to know, although usually the government goes after the bigger companies and not the little ones.

One onerous U.S. regulation concerns your ability to declare your price is discounted from a previous (higher) price. The government has very specific requirements (that still, somehow contain "murkiness"!) as to how long you had to offer your product/service at the higher price in order to now declare it reduced. Most small companies ignore this regulation (or don't know about it), but the government did sue Macy's over this very regulation and won a big settlement.

The United States also has a number of laws about price discrimination—limiting your ability to give price breaks to one group or business compared to others—and price fixing.

If you're planning to sell outside the United States, pricing regulations can get even murkier. For example, Europe has one set of pricing regulations for most firms, but a different standard for the leading competitor in each field.

If you can afford it, you should talk to an attorney who has handled pricing law as it affects your industry. As at least a first step, you can often talk your industry associations into having presentations from attorneys on marketing and pricing laws and regulations.

Social Trends

Social trends can have a strong impact on the price you command. For example, let's look at the frozen food industry. For decades, consumers who bought frozen dinners did so with a great emphasis on price. But then two social trends led the way to higher price possibilities:

1. Cocooning. As people started staying home more instead of going out to eat, they were willing to buy a better-quality frozen dinner. After all, they were comparing the price of it to the price of dinning out, instead of the price of preparing the meal from scratch.

2. Back-to-nature. As more people became concerned about artificial chemicals used to enhance or preserve flavor, consumers became willing to pay higher prices for food (including frozen dinners) without those additives.

The same trends may also impact the business-to-business (B2B) marketplace. If consumers are buying more and more of a particular product, at healthy profit margins, the manufacturers of those products are under a greater compulsion to grow than to cut their costs. That means if you manufacture packaging for frozen foods, your customers may allow higher prices in return for faster and more reliable response time.

There are a number of firms that chart social trends, most of which charge very big money for their services. But if you Google "social trends America 2012" you will find a number of companies who have published some of their research.

For example, as of July 2012:

1. Two highlights from the Pew Institute include:

    a. The rise of Asian Americans, and

    b. The social division between Republicans and Democrats now has a values gap greater than that between gender, age, race, or class.

2. Forrester calls attention to the growth in mobile device usage, and—for retail establishments—the trend to web retailing and the greatly increasing competition from Amazon.com.

3. JWT Intelligence forecasts:

    a. Consumers are tired of scrimping and looking for more (albeit small) indulgences,

    b. More and more Americans will be starting their own businesses,

    c. Food will become the new eco-issue, and

    d. Women are increasingly deciding not to marry.

How does all this affect pricing?

- New products appealing to the leading edge of a trend can often command higher prices. (For example, frozen dinners have finally gone gourmet—offering much better choices for a single woman or man wanting gourmet food at home quickly and easily.)

- Products/services where demand is (or will be) shrinking often find themselves in a battle for survival—where prices will most usually shrink.

- How is your industry doing on the social front? A half hour spent searching for consumer trends might cause you to raise or lower your price—and therefore profit—opportunities.

Technological Change

Technological change, even in products other than your own, can affect your company's pricing and sales. For example, I was publisher of *Audio* magazine for CBS when the music industry was switching from LPs to CDs. It was a great time for the magazine because most companies in the industry wanted to advertise their new (usually higher priced) products. It wasn't just the sale of CD players and CDs themselves to replace your LP music collection. It was also sales of better (higher-priced) amplifiers and car music systems.

There are two downsides to this phenomenon:

1. Even if you're on the uptrend of new technology, competitors will quickly drive down the prices. Your pricing plans for any new technology of your own should be to very quickly recoup any R&D (research and development) expenses you have, plus your launch expenses.

   Example: Gillette spent over $750 million developing the Mach 3, which was quickly supplanted by razors with even more blades. Gillette had to earn back their research and development costs quickly in the price they set at the launch.

2. There's nothing pretty about the price you can command for yesterday's hot technology anything. While some industries will allow you to continue selling a last-generation product for a long time, the price you can command for it will inevitably be driven down.

Further, if you're in a technology-driven industry, the time line for you to recoup costs and pocket profits is getting smaller and smaller. That means you need to price high enough to earn all the profits you can in the expected growth and maturity phases of the life cycle of your product. Once a competitor supersedes your invention, your goal will change to being able to sell off your remaining inventory—driving your price down quickly and sharply.

CHAPTER 5

Pick the Positioning of Your New Product

In-a-Rush Tip

This chapter is critical. You need to read it all!

There Are Only 3 Choices!

There are only three positioning strategies for your prices—but enormous complexities within each.

Your options are only:

1. Lower than your competitors (penetration pricing)

2. Higher than your competitors (skimming pricing)

3. Roughly the same as your competitors (competitive pricing)

How do you determine the best price for your new offering? You must first understand the psychology of your price positioning.

Warning

Sometimes the best position is simply *the one that is open*. For example, if you're planning to launch a new barbeque sauce and the competitors are all priced about the same, that tells you the best position for your new product may be premium priced. If lots of people are buying barbeque sauce, some of them are likely to pay an extra dollar for a better sauce. That extra dollar will cover your extra costs and give you a nicer profit margin. Plus when you launch, your unique selling proposition (USP) is easy and compelling: "Treat yourself to the BEST!"

The Psychology of Price Positioning

It is critical to understand what a price conveys to consumers about your product. One of the biggest mistakes you see with new marketers is a disconnect between the product positioning and the price.

If you want your product to be perceived as one of the best quality choices among your competitors, you can't have the lowest price. Period! By the same token, if you have the lowest price (or one of the lowest prices), consumers will refuse to believe your product is high quality. Yes, if you have a well-known, quality brand name and then have a low price, consumers will not infer low quality. (Although if the price is low enough, they may suspect it's a knockoff.) But especially for new brands or moderately known brand names,

the price you put on your product is a key indicator to consumers of its quality.

The consumer doesn't know your brand. (Even if you've been around for a while, many to most won't know what your brand stands for.) They don't know what quality standards you have or haven't implemented.

But they know that *you* know. You know better than anyone the quality of your product. So if you put a low price on it, the consumer will believe you know that a low price is all it's worth. If you put a higher price on it, the consumer will believe you know that a high price is what it's worth.

But . . . keep in mind that the consumer is not an idiot. If you price high but the consumer can tell (either before *or* after purchase) that your materials are substandard, you will pay a steep price for your deception. That price could be low sales, high returns (if the quality is evident only after purchase), and/or a high trashing of your product on Internet review sites.

I have conducted research on the pricing of a new HDTV brand, where I found that good consumer reviews were every bit as valuable to a new product as a good brand name. They have become the new gold standard for quality assurance!

Penetration Price Positioning

Most new business owners default to penetration price positioning (pricing lower than their competitors) because they are afraid nobody will buy their product otherwise.

Let's be clear about this. You will likely (but certainly not always!) have a lot more sales if you select this option. The question is: Will you be more profitable—or a lot less profitable?

And also, this is the most *dangerous* price positioning you can assume, and in a minute I'll show you why.

But first . . .

Two Situations that Call for Penetration Pricing

Who *should* use penetration pricing? Anyone in one of these two situations:

1. New product or service launches where the product/service gains value only when it has large numbers of buyers/users.

    Examples:

    - You are launching the first fax machine. A fax machine is worthless unless other people have them. If not, who will you fax to?

    - You are launching Facebook. Facebook had little value at first; the value comes from lots of your friends all having Facebook pages.

    These types of products or services require a large base of customers/users before they have real value. In this case, a price of free (Facebook) or very low (a first fax machine) will help you increase value to your offering. In fact, fax machines took decades before they had many buyers—because the first ones were not priced using penetration pricing.

2. Anyone who has costs that are *sustainably* 30 percent or more lower than their competitors. If you're in this position, penetration pricing is great. What you need to do is explain your lower costs to the marketplace—so they'll not infer poor quality by your prices, but understand you can price lower because your costs are lower.

Examples:

- A graphics designer based in rural Tennessee. His costs were much lower than those of most designers, based in New York or other large cities. He promoted his services by the line "New York Quality—at Tennessee Prices!" Potential customers could immediately understand why his prices could be so low—without it being due to quality.

- Wal-Mart. You can't talk about penetration pricing without talking about Wal-Mart. If you ask any consumer today why Wal-Mart prices are so much lower, they will tell you it's because Wal-Mart buys in such large quantity, and many will also tell you it's because they squeeze their vendors and they pay poor wages and benefits to their employees. Oh . . . and they also carry some poor-quality brands, along with better ones. (See the section below under "How to Avoid a Price War" for how smart Wal-Mart was when they first launched.)

Two Reasons to *Not* Use Penetration Pricing

There are a lot of negatives when it comes to penetration pricing. For example, in a NewProd model developed by Cooper (1985), the results imply that penetration pricing is a fallback option that is inferior to product superiority and to be used only if the company can't obtain superiority and have it fit within the company. He found lower pricing than competitors to be fourth in economic advantage to the company, behind:

1. Product superiority, quality, and uniqueness
2. The fit between the product and the company, in terms of knowledge, skills, and resources
3. Market need, growth, and size

I believe there are two major reasons not to use penetration pricing, which are detailed here.

Reason #1: To Avoid a Perception of Poor Quality

If you see a very low price on a pair of Nikes, what do you think? If it's low but possible, you probably think "Great deal!" and want to buy them. If the price is unreasonably low, you probably think "Bet they're poor-quality knockoffs." Same with any well-known and respected brand name.

But when you launch a new product or service or when you have a brand that doesn't have millions of dollars spent promoting the name, you don't get the "Great deal!" benefit of the doubt. A low price on an unknown brand is almost always perceived as being due to a lower quality.

For example, I was shocked to find I got 11 percent *more* orders for my business newsletter at $127 than I got at $97. But upon further reflection, it's perfectly logical. Most business newsletters (although none of them were direct competitors) were priced at $150–$399 when I launched. My price of $97 looked surprisingly low. Surprisingly low equals poor quality perception. Once I raised my price to a more "normal" amount, the low-quality-perception-due-to-price stopped being a factor.

This quality perception is a much bigger problem in some categories than in others.

- *Example #1*: Suppose you see lots of laundry detergent products at $2.99, and one in a comparable size at $2.25. Would you buy the $2.25 brand? Maybe. Maybe not.

- *Example #2*: Suppose you are on trial for a murder you didn't commit. Most of the attorneys you contact charge $450/hour. One attorney wants $199/hour. They all have good recommendations. Would you hire the $199/hour attorney? Not if there was any way in hell you could find the money for one of the others!

- *Example #3*: Suppose you want to get a face lift. You get quotes from plastic surgeons with good credentials and recommendations of $10,000, $9,500, $11,000,

and $6,999. Again, there's little likelihood of you selecting the $6,999 surgeon if there's any way you can afford one of the others.

What will happen to your customers if your product turns out to be poor quality? A bad box of detergent? So what? A bad criminal attorney? A death sentence. If the risk is great, the likelihood of a successful low pricing strategy is lower. If the risk is minimal, the quality perceptions can be managed with ads and/or product packaging that stress quality.

Reason #2: To Prevent a Price War

If you under-price the current products in your marketplace, you will likely start a price war with your competitors. Starting a price war is another junior-marketer mistake. It comes from planning your own strategy without considering what reactions your competitors will have to your pricing. If those competitors think you have a chance of success, you can bet the farm they *will* respond in some manner.

Price War Example   Suppose you plan to enter a competitive marketplace, and the current prices of your soon-to-be competitors are:

- $35
- $31

- $29
- $27

Your costs are $20, so you decide to enter the market with a price of $26. What do you think the competitors will do?

Consider your competitor at $27. The market positioning of that competitor is "lowest price." That's what that company is known for—how customers see it. If you take away that "lowest-price" position from that competitor, what does it have left? Probably nothing. It certainly wasn't competing on quality, so you've left it probably with no positioning.

Think of your lowest-price competitor as if it were the Wal-Mart of your industry. The only reason you buy at Wal-Mart is to get lower prices (and sometimes convenience and one-stop shopping). If you opened a store that competed with Wal-Mart by offering lower prices, what do you think Wal-Mart would do?

That $27 competitor is most likely to drop its price to $25 in order to remain the lowest-priced competitor. What is your response? If you want to be the lowest-priced option, you'll drop your price to $24. Then it will drop to $23, then you drop to $22, then it drops to $21.

Now you have a terrible problem. You can't lower your price anymore and still make any profit at all. So you're stuck at a $22 price—and you are *not* the lowest-priced offering.

The hard truth is that the $27 competitor could probably go lower than you and still have a profit because it already has economies of scale. If you're making $2 profit at a $22 price, it will probably be making more than that at a $21 price. But that's not the biggest problem.

After this price war, you are *not* the lowest-priced product—and you're making only $2 per unit sold. If you had been smart and entered the market at $28, one dollar above the lowest-priced competitor, you'd still not be the lowest-priced product—but you'd be making $8 profit per unit sold.

If you're not going to end up being the low-cost competitor, it's better to be second lowest at a higher price than second lowest at a rock-bottom price.

If you can't win a price war, don't start one!

How to Avoid a Price War—If You Really Do Have 30 Percent Lower Costs

One of the smartest moves Wal-Mart ever made was at its launch. Wal-Mart had invested millions of dollars in automated warehousing and in a whole just-in-time inventory system where vendors have to ship small amounts frequently (costing the vendors more money, but saving money for Wal-Mart). In addition, Wal-Mart didn't "buy" from many vendors until the product was sold in their stores. Those vendors have to ship product which Wal-Mart will either buy from them as it sells, or return to them if it doesn't.

In other words, Wal-Mart's costs were at least 30 percent lower than its potential competitors, and those competitors couldn't easily match Wal-Mart's costs without huge investments.

But what if the competitors didn't realize this? What if, when Wal-Mart launched, its competitors started a price war with Wal-Mart? Yes, Wal-Mart could have "won" the war—but at the end of it, prices would have been much lower than those Wal-Mart could charge without a price war.

Remember, no company really "wins" a price war. One company will emerge from such a war holding the low-price position, but its profits will be greatly reduced. Because once you've lowered your prices for a product, it's very, very hard (often impossible) to raise them back up when the war is over. If consumers have learned that you can buy product X for $15, then you raise it back to $21, you'll find your sales will disappear!

So how did Wal-Mart avoid a ruinous price war when it launched? Remember, it's illegal to talk to your competitors about pricing!

Instead, Wal-Mart gave lots of interviews to the business magazines. Those interviews talked about Wal-Mart's state-of-the-art equipment and systems—that other companies don't have. Wal-Mart let its competitors know just how much lower its costs were, so the competitors would not start a price war. The hidden message of those interviews was this:

"Don't even *think* about starting a price war with us because our costs are so much lower than yours that we'll be dancing on your graves!"

Skimming (or Premium) Price Positioning

Companies that have the highest price positions in a marketplace are usually smaller, with less sales than companies that price lower. But they are usually some of the most profitable companies. Example: Timex sells more watches and probably has higher dollar sales, but for profits we'd both have more cash if we owned Rolex!

There is a lot of research on a higher price equaling higher quality in buyers' minds (which you'll see in Chapter 14).

Here it's worth noting that buyers see a quality difference—even if it doesn't exist! Here are three studies where a higher price all by itself makes the product more attractive.

Beer Study

Beer drinkers prefer the taste of beers that are priced higher—even if the blind taste test uses the same beer!

McConnell (1968) did blind taste tests using the same beer and got these results.

- He was especially impressed with the anger and hostility beer taste-testers showed when told there was no difference in the beers they tasted. He sees this as proof that they did indeed perceive quality differences in the beers that were due entirely to and positively correlated with the price.

Carpet Study

- Carpet buyers can be repelled by low prices—even if their senses should be telling them the quality is good. Gabor and Granger (1966) found that even consumers handed a carpet sample, so they could ascertain the quality for themselves, were uninterested in buying it if the price was low.

- They handed buyers a sample of a quality carpet that normally sold at 72 shillings per square yard. Here's how likely they were to buy when given an artificially low price:

  - 60 percent likely when told the price was 40–60 shillings

  - 30 percent likely, when told the price was 20–40 shillings

Wine Study

- Neuroeconomists at Caltech conducted a very revealing study about wines. They revealed that our brains themselves tell us an expensive wine tastes better than a cheap wine, even if—unknown to us—the two wines are the same!

- They hooked up wine tasters to equipment showing brain activity. When tasters were told the wine was $45, one additional area of the brain was stimulated—the orbitofrontal cortex—and the tasters reported a better taste. When told the same wine was $5, that portion of the brain was not excited, and tasters reported a much poorer taste.

Net Result

Tasters actually—physically as well as mentally!—got more pleasure from drinking an expensive wine than from a cheaper wine—even though they were both the same. The premium-price position in most (not all) industries is the most profitable.

There are two types of skimming pricing:

1. Temporary premium

2. Prestige pricing

Temporary Premium Pricing

A temporary skimming/premium price strategy works best for unique products, or those with a clear (usually technological) benefit over the competitors. The price is set high at the launch, because either the product has no competitors or it is demonstrably better.

But you do expect competitors to arrive and/or improve their products to become comparable to yours. Once competitors catch up, it is expected that your price will be lowered to end up in the same ballpark as your competitors.

Why is this done? For three reasons:

1. To recoup your research and development (R&D) costs. For example, Gillette spent $750 million in R&D to develop the Gillette Mach 3. The company needs to recoup this investment, and the only time it can is when the product gives it a lead in the market that consumers will pay more for.

2. To protect company profits. Multiproduct companies have a mix of products, some with high profits, some moderate, and some that are losing money. A company needs fat profits on some products to support the products that are (for the moment) losing money—perhaps because they are in the process of being launched.

3. Because you can. If you have developed a unique or demonstrably better product, then you deserve the rewards of your efforts. That's our capitalist system.

Prestige Pricing

A prestige pricing strategy is where you decide to have the best quality and highest (or one of the highest) priced products in a market. A luxury product.

What's a luxury product? It isn't determined by the actual dollar price of the product; it's the price relative to your competitors. There's a luxury brand of bubble bath and luxury cookies. It's all relative.

Look at your industry. If all your competitors are priced about the same, there may be a position open for a "luxury" brand in your marketplace—one that justifies its higher price through better quality ingredients, "green" ingredients, "natural" ingredients, classier packaging, etc.

This is a great, highly profitable strategy—unless there's already a brand in your market that "owns" the prestige position. For example, Sony used to own the prestige position in consumer electronics products—and still does with some consumers although their problems have eroded this perception.

However, there could be a prestige position that is even higher than the one owned by a brand. Example: Rolex is the prestige brand for most of us when considering a watch to buy. However, there are some brands much more expensive for a different target group of customers—those who think a Rolex is too ordinary.

We'll cover pricing psychology in detail in Chapter 11, but I want to make sure you note here that prestige products typically are not priced in pennies. For example, a $14.99 price makes a product look "ordinary" or discounted, whereas a price of $14 or $15 conveys high-quality.

For example, there are a lot of consumer health newsletters, most priced around $19.99, some at $29.99. The point is, they all have pennies in their prices. Harvard publishes a number of consumer health newsletters itself. Their prices are $22, $24, or $28. No pennies.

I have seen "luxury" brands include pennies in their prices (especially electronics), but I strongly recommend you test a price without them. Luxury is part image, after all, and pennies don't fit the image.

Competitive Price Positioning

The third price positioning option is competitive. That means you price in the ballpark of your competitors.

This strategy hasn't received much attention/respect from pricing researchers due to it being confused with a "match-competitor-pricing" strategy, which is actually quite different

- "Match-competitor prices" is a strategy that requires no investigation of the best price. You just pick a price similar to competitors and run with it. It is substantially better than a cost-plus pricing strategy, but that's like saying a punch in the face is better than getting maimed. Yeah, it is. But why would you want either?

Warning

There is a limit to how high a quality you can deliver and still reap the rewards in pricing. A friend of mine makes luxury bed linens sold in upscale department stores. She buys gazillion-thread-count luxury cloth to make the linens, but she doesn't buy the best cloth possible. She would like to go with the absolute best, but she's found there's an upper limit to what people will pay for bed linens—even very rich people.

- A competitive pricing strategy is the end result of an analysis of your competitors and their products' benefits and negatives, as well as an analysis of what customers want from products in your category.

Among companies that do not use cost-plus as their pricing strategy, competitive price positioning is the next most utilized, probably because it requires the least amount of time investment.

Reasons to Use a Competitive Price Positioning Strategy

There are a number of reasons for selecting this strategy over a premium/prestige-position or a penetration/low-positioning strategy. Some are:

- Because the high priced position(s) is/are already owned by strong competitor(s)
- Because you don't have the lower costs necessary for a successful low-price positioning
- Because customers in your category don't care for a luxury version (e.g., it's detergent and the market for luxury detergent is too small or nonexistent)
- Because customers in your category care much more about some other factor than price (e.g., convenience, terms, celebrity endorsement, etc.)

It is important to note that companies who successfully use a competitive price positioning will find themselves competing on something other than price.

The Lazy Person's Guide to Pricing Strategy

1. Most popular: cost-plus pricing. Calculate costs, then slap a profit margin on top of it. (See Chapter 2 for all the ways this hurts marketers.)
2. Second most popular: match-competitors pricing. Pick a price similar to competitors and run with it. (See earlier in this chapter for how this differs from a more optimal competitive pricing strategy.)

Learning More about Competitive Pricing

Is competitor benchmarking more critical for retail-sold products, which are displayed close to competitive products? One indication this may be true is the price differential between books sold in retail stores (including online stores) and e-books sold individually online. Individually sold e-books carry disproportionately higher prices per page than do printed books, even though pricing on a cost-plus basis would produce the opposite result.

In studying successful new-product pricing practices, Ingenbleek et al. (2003) found competition-informed (or based) pricing was:

- Successful in highly competitive markets when relative product advantage is low

- Unsuccessful in highly competitive markets when you have a high relative product advantage

  - That's because companies in their study appeared to underestimate the value of their innovative products.

- They also found competitive-based pricing to be of less value when competition is strong. They postulate it is due to quick competitive matching of any innovative differences, causing a downward spiral in pricing. In such a situation, companies that do not pay attention to their cost floors may find themselves making unprofitable pricing decisions.

Exporters in the United Kingdom were surveyed by Tzokas et al. (2000), who found prices were set by these exporters based primarily upon production costs, foreign customer needs, and then competitive price levels.

Noble and Gruca (1999):

- Classified competitive pricing (including leader, parity, and low-price positions) as appropriate only for mature products. They did, however, note a Harvard Business School case (Shapiro, 1977) where the optimal pricing for a new product required competitive and product line pricing considerations.

- Found that parity pricing was most used by firms with high costs, low market shares, low product differentiation, and high levels of capacity utilization and brand elasticity.

- Found that unlike any of the other pricing strategies, the importance weight given for this strategy by those using it was split. While the median was 50 percent, almost half of the managers rated it much higher or lower—outside the middle of the scale (30 percent–80 percent).

  - This may be reflecting two different kinds of companies using this strategy: those that considered competitive prices only in passing, and those for which a competitive price positioning was an essential part of their pricing and marketing strategy.

Cannon and Morgan (1990) considered "going-rate" pricing inappropriate if there are not a number of close substitute products on the market.

Zais (1977) found competitive pricing was the most used pricing strategy for information centers and libraries when initiating user fees. He found it ideal for centers that had insufficient cost data with which to price their services and that also had little information on demand.

CHAPTER 6

Analyzing Your Buyer Benefits/ Drawbacks Relative to Your Competitors

In-a-Rush Tip

This chapter is critical. Read it all and complete this chapter's worksheet on at least some of your competitors. **If you sell to consumers,** you need to complete Part 1 of the workbook. **If you sell to businesses,** you need to complete Parts 1 and 2. Please note: If you limit the number of competitors you analyze, you may miss key benefits you could add to your product/service.

At a minimum, you need to understand what benefits users get from each aspect of your competitors' products or services versus what they get from you.

Benefits are *not* features. Features need to be translated to: *What's in it for the customer? And it must be from the customer's point of view, not yours!*

Examples:

- Feature: "100 more MB of RAM"

  - Benefit: "Cuts your wait time because it runs three times faster"

- Feature: "Waterproof" mascara

  - Benefit: "Won't run down your face"

- Feature: "Condensed"

  - Benefit: "We've cut all the fluff, so you get all the important content in half the time."

- Feature: "Half the calories"

  - Benefit: "Eat twice as much without gaining a pound!"

  - Benefit: "Eat what you normally do—and still lose weight!"

- Feature: "24/7 customer support"

  - Benefit: "Your job is safe with us! If something goes wrong, we'll fix it any time any day!"

List your competitors' names across the columns. Should you take the time to fill in details for more than your closest two or three competitors? Yes, because it may uncover opportunities for you to add a lot more profits to your bottom line!

The more benefits you find that others are offering, the better you can understand what a buyer is looking for with your type of product. Some benefits offered by others may be ones you can add into your product for little or no additional costs.

The "negatives" section is also critical. Especially if you take a little extra effort and try to imagine yourself in the shoes of one or more of your buyer types. Imagine them deciding which brand to buy. Imagine them using one of the products for the first time.

- What would annoy them?

- What would confuse them?

- What kind of extra effort are they being forced to use to enjoy the product? Effort that perhaps you could remove from your offering.

Uncovering What Buyers *Really* Value/ Hate about Products in Your Marketplace

To take this next critical step in setting your prices, go to the Chapter 6 Buyer Benefits Worksheet in this book's Appendix.

Learn More about Calculating Buyer *Valuation* of Different Features

Calculating the value of features that differ from competitors is one of the most difficult parts of setting a new product/ service price.

Consider a 5 percent increase in the effectiveness of a bar of soap. It is probably that customers will see no value in this addition, and be unwilling to pay a higher price. Consider, alternatively, a 5 percent improvement in the effectiveness of a wrinkle-removing cream. Consumer valuation of this improvement may be 100 percent or 200 percent higher than current products.

This problem also exists in pricing pharmaceuticals. Drugs that increase the therapeutic gains of existing drugs were able to command two or three times the price of existing drugs, despite their relative therapeutic advantage being nowhere near that proportion (Lu and Comanor, 1998).

An interesting research study by Udell and Potter (1989) found attributes in new technology to be licensed to others influence the royalty rate that can be charged. Given a normal royalty rate of between 0.5 and 15 percent of sales, the researchers found nine factors can help determine how high or low within that range the price should fall. Those factors included the importance of the invention, the strength of the patent/trade secret, the competitive structure of the marketplace, investment required for commercialization, stage of development for the technology (the further along it is, the less the risk), the competitive advantage of it, the profit margin available, the extent of the innovation, and the terms (which include exclusivity and any advance payments required).

Researchers Sapede and Girod (2002) developed a conjoint model that varied price, attribute levels, and duration of protection for a vaccine. They found price was by far the most important attribute tested, in each of two countries, with roughly equal utility scores. However, the countries were very different in price elasticity. In one country, small changes in price created large changes in willingness to buy, while the other country showed much less change in demand for different price levels.

Undergraduate students in Florida and Pennsylvania were offered 18 different credit card choices (each with a different array of attributes) to determine the optimal features for a card targeting this market. The researchers found that the interest rate and the type of payment (i.e., deferred payment options) were the most important. Further, they found different attributes of differing interest to the target customers based on gender. Females were more interested in the American Express brand name, whereas males were more interested in extended payment options (Kara, Kaynak and Kucukemiroglu, 1994).

One note of caution: If you have very different groups of buyers, you may not be able to find a single value for an attribute; the groups may differ widely. For example, Hogan (2005) found a medical device manufacturer that developed a new tool that could speed up certain clinical tests by tenfold. Despite rave reviews, the product sales fell substantially short of expectations. A consultant determined that the tool saved pharmaceutical companies a lot of money and could be priced much higher to this group. However, university buyers found the improvements a negative, as it reduced student learning of testing procedures.

Your Assignment

Fill out the Buyer Benefits Worksheet today!

CHAPTER 7

Picking a "Ballpark" for Your Best Price

In-a-Rush Tip

This chapter is critical. You need to read it all!

In this chapter, we start to winnow down the pricing choices to a range that would be most effective for your new product or service.

To do this, look at your Competitor Pricing Worksheet (Chapter 3) and your Buyer Benefits Worksheet (Chapter 6) in this book's Appendix. Then visit the companion web site, download/print out the worksheets, and put them beside your computer.

The key decision for this chapter is the price position you *want* to have. Your choices follow. If you have questions on which to select, review the three positions in greater detail in Chapter 5.

- Penetration Pricing
  - Use penetration pricing if your costs are definitely 30 percent or more *lower* than your competitors—*and* it would be hard for them to match your costs.

- Use penetration pricing if you want to be one of the cheaper products on the marketplace.

- Use penetration pricing if you will have fewer benefits (or more negatives) than most of your competitors.

- Skimming or Prestige Pricing

  - Use skimming pricing if your new product is *very* different from your competitors and offers benefits none of the others offer.

  - Use skimming pricing if you have large R&D costs to recoup and your new product is different enough that consumers will pay a premium for it.

  - Use prestige (permanently higher) pricing if your product is of higher quality/benefit to consumers than the competitors.

  - Use prestige pricing if your product will appeal to a smaller group of customers willing to pay more for a better product/service.

- Competitive Pricing

  - Use competitive pricing if your benefits and negatives do not stand out strongly from those of your competitors.

  - Use competitive pricing if the other two strategies won't work for you because:

    - Your costs aren't 30 percent or more lower than your competitors.

    - Your quality/benefits aren't at the top of your competitors.

- Use competitive pricing because you are going to compete on *one* something other than price. Examples:

  - Fastest service

  - Fun colors (appeals to a younger group)

  - Better for a subset of buyers

    - For example, you sell swim goggles and you come out with a benefit specifically for triathletes. Note: Being the first choice for a subset of buyers is a more profitable position than being a so-so choice for the larger group of buyers.

  - Customizable

You Will Not Be "Stuck" with Your Decision!

Don't let indecision paralyze you at this point! Pick the one of the three you feel in your gut is best. But know that you will be able to change it (rather easily!) in later chapters if the profits aren't what you want.

The value of starting at this point is it lets you see the ramifications of this decision. That way, if it causes problems you'll discover them *before* they become reality. You'll discover them when you can easily change to something that will work better for you.

Pick the one position you think might be best for you and enter it in the Chapter 7 Narrowing Your Price Range Worksheet (see the Appendix, but also the companion web site). When finished, check out your profits.

Can't Make a Profit at that Price Range?

If you already know (given your costs) that you can't make a profit with a price in this range, you've saved yourself from a pricing disaster! You now know you can't make it with the price position you thought was best.

That means you have to try a different price position, which also means you have to reconsider questions of quality, service, etc. Typically this result occurs when you want to enter in a penetration pricing strategy, then realize you really can't compete on the low end and have enough profits to earn a living.

Go back and re-do the Chapter 7 worksheet, this time putting in different competitors at your different price positioning strategy. Just make sure you plan your benefits and negatives to be comparable to your new group of competitors!

Not Sure about Your Results?

Don't worry; most people aren't. That's why the next chapter (Chapter 8) will guide you through learning whether or not you can make a profit with this particular price positioning strategy.

Why didn't that chapter come earlier? Because the worst pricing mistake you can make is to get your costs, tack on a profit margin, and blindly assume people will be willing to

Your Assignment

Complete the worksheet now. Don't worry—it won't take much time at all, because you will use the material you already compiled from the Chapter 3 and Chapter 6 worksheets.

When you are finished, ask yourself: How do you like your projected price range?

buy it. (See more on the problems with cost-plus pricing in Chapter 2.)

Instead, you have taken the time to learn what buyers are willing to pay for products with different types of benefits and negatives in *your* marketplace.

Now, when we look at costs, you'll learn if you can make money with the benefits and negatives you were planning to offer. If not, you'll be able to reconsider your benefits and negatives—*before* wasting any money trying to sell something buyers won't buy.

Learn More about Buyers' Reactions to Price Ranges

There's some very interesting research on establishing "ranges" for pricing. This is especially critical when offering buyers a range of prices—typically found when asking for donations.

Soliciting Donations

Is there a difference in the amount donated—based on the "suggested donations" you list? Desmet (1999) found it depends on which suggestions you manipulate. Suppose you offer the following "suggested donations":

- $15
- $30
- $50
- $75
- $100

Desmet's research suggests that changing the $30, $50, or $75 will have little effect, but raising the top or the bottom number will have significant results.

In his research, raising the top number led to overall larger donations. Strangely, raising the bottom number led to significantly lower response rates. Why would raising the $15 cause fewer people to donate? The dropoff came from previous donors who had contributed a small amount. Desmet cites an "aversion to the extremes," whereby donors do not want to contribute the smallest or the largest amount on the list.

So adding a $125 choice would increase the number of people who would donate $100. But if the lowest number shown becomes $30, then people who donated $30 before would now be donating the lowest amount listed—which they don't want to do. Instead, some of them may choose not to donate.

Buyers' Assimilation or Contrasting of Prices

When consumers see an advertised price that is close to their internal reference price, they assimilate it. An advertised price that is too far away from what they expect is contrasted—and thus discounted (Sherif and Hovland, 1964).

This assimilation/contrast theory also shows that buyers judge the range of advertised prices they face by the extreme values. For example, Oxenfeldt (1973) found the prices most noticed by buyers are the highest and the lowest. They also found in the middle of the range a "latitude of acceptance." That means that an advertised price that is close to the expected reference price is within those latitudes of acceptance and is thus accepted.

Compeau and Grewal (1998) created a model of reference price processing based upon assimilation-contrast theory. In their model, the advertised reference price ("Was $XX") and the advertised selling price ("Now $X") both affect consumers, who must decide if they are believable and acceptable. If so, they assimilate the price (perhaps with some discounting of the "Was" price) and it becomes their new reference price.

If the advertised reference price is not acceptable or believable, then the consumer contrasts it. In both cases, the consumer then compares his or her current internal reference price to the advertised sale price to form a perception of the advertised deal's value.

However, most researchers (Krishnan et al., 2006; Biswas et al., 1999; Suter and Burton, 1996; Licata, Biswas, and Krishnan, 1998; Compeau, Grewal, and Chandrashekaran, 2002) have found that even implausible reference prices can affect internal reference prices. These researchers found that implausibly high advertised prices may be met with skepticism and a discounting of the discount, but they still cause consumers to accept higher prices as being in the normal range (not as high as the implausibly high advertised price, but still higher than would have happened without seeing the ad).

PART 3

Your Cost Analysis

n this section, you will develop your direct costs for your product or service as well as your "fully loaded" costs, which include overhead.

You need this to provide a "floor" for your range of potential prices.

CHAPTER 8

Evaluating Your Costs

In-a-Rush Tip

Do *not* skip this critical chapter or the Cost Analysis Worksheet for it. (See the Appendix and also visit the companion web site to download/print out the worksheet.) However, if your costs do not change with the quantity you sell, you can skip the part of the worksheet that deals with quantity/cost changes.

The Ideas Behind "Target Costing" and "Target Engineering"

The traditional cost-plus calculation gives way to a more market-oriented, price-minus calculation. The amount customers are willing to pay for a product that fulfills their requirements is determined first. Based on this information, the highest acceptable price is calculated, and the target margin is deducted from that price. The result is the maximum cost allowable for this product. The traditional idea of "How much will the product cost?" is replaced with "How much can the product cost?"

Butscher and Laker (2000)

JUMP had a new basketball sneaker with several advanced features and a modified cushioning technology. The cost of the sneaker was $40. Adding the target margin of 100 percent resulted in a price to the dealer of $80. Adding the dealer's margin of 50 percent on top of that led to a market price of $120, which put this sneaker in the upper price range with the most expensive models from Adidas, Nike, and Reebok. Expected sales in this price category were thin.

... JUMP decided to reevaluate the new shoe using the target-costing approach. It was discovered that the target segments preferred a less elaborate shoe. The maximum acceptable price for such a shoe was determined to be $99, just under the $100 price step, which positioned the JUMP sneaker at a slight price premium to most other basketball sneakers price in the $70-$90 range. The new features the JUMP sneaker had justified this price premium. Deducting the 50% dealer margin led to a price to the dealer of $66. Deducting the 100% target margin from that price resulted in a target cost for the sneaker of $33, which was $7 lower than the current cost. JUMP was able to slash the cost to $33 by slightly redesigning the sneaker to lower the production cost and by optimizing transportation from the Asian production plan to the distribution centers globally. It launched the sneaker nine months after the original target date. (Butscher and Laker, 2000)

It was a success, but not as big as it could have been if it made the target date and could have been promoted at the Dream Team Olympics in Atlanta. That could have happened, had they started with target costing.

Types of Costs

There are three different types of costs to analyze for this section of the book:

1. Sunk costs

2. Overhead costs

3. Direct costs

Let's look at each type.

Sunk Costs

Sunk costs are those costs needed to launch a company—or a new product. They include costs such as establishing a new dealer network, researching the new industry, researching new competitors, preparing financial and sales projections, etc.

There are tax implications (the IRS requires some of these costs to be capitalized, not expensed) as to what you classify as sunk costs.

For the purposes of setting prices *only*, consider sunk costs to be those up to manufacturing and selling costs. In other words, sunk costs are what you spend setting up the company and procedures so you can then either start manufacturing and/or start selling.

Overhead Costs

Overhead costs are those ongoing costs that will not go away if you change the products or services you are offering. They are divided into two groups and include costs such as:

- Administrative costs
  - Rent
  - Utilities

- Salary and benefits of positions that would not go away if you changed what you sell. These include the CEO, CFO, CIO, administrative assistants, and other administrators.

- Sales-related management costs (not specific to any product or service)

  - These include the chief marketing officer's (CMO's) salary and benefits, plus any overall research or marketing services and/or databases you buy that aren't specific to one product or service you offer.

Direct Costs

Direct costs are those that are directly required for manufacture of or provision of specific products or services. Examples include:

- Blank t-shirts and colored inks, if you sell imprinted t-shirts. And salary and benefits for any employees who work imprinting the t-shirts.

- Attorney costs, if you run a legal firm.

- Hair stylist expenses (employees plus shampoos, conditioners, etc.) if you run a hair salon.

- Writer fees (or salaries), photo fees, printing expenses, and postage/delivery fees to mail issues if you have a magazine, newspaper, or newsletter.

The Hardest Part of Calculating Costs

The most difficult aspect of calculating your costs is deciding what amount of your sunk costs and/or overhead costs to add in when calculating your total costs for a product.

There are a few methods of calculating your total costs for pricing purposes:

- What are your direct costs per unit?

- How many other products/services are you offering that can carry part of the overhead?

- Is the upside for this product/service worth it contributing less-than-optimal dollars to overhead for some time at its introduction?

If your price at least covers direct costs, the company is making at least some money that can be applied to overhead.

Let's look at an example:

- Your direct costs for this product are $12 per unit.

- Let's assume your "fully loaded" costs are $20 per unit. (This covers a percentage of overhead applied to each unit based on total overhead costs divided by the number of units of this and other products you expect to sell.)

- Then let's assume your previous market analysis shows competitor products that are equivalent to yours are selling for $19 per unit.

- Should you go ahead with the launch?

Over the long haul, you need to make more than enough to cover your overhead. So if you think this is the total upside for this product and it won't aid you in other ways to be described below, then no—launching it wouldn't be smart.

However, it will be contributing $9 per unit sold to overhead. So if you don't launch it, you lose $9 on each non-sale toward overhead.

Reasons for Launching a Product that Doesn't Cover Overhead

You may well wish to launch a product where the price does cover direct costs but doesn't cover all the indirect (overhead) costs. Here are some valid reasons:

- It's an entry into an industry that is attractive to you.

- It's an entry product that will bring in customers, many of which will upgrade to your higher margin products/services.

- It's a product that requires additional products with a higher margin. For example:

  - Pricing razors cheap because the profit margins on the blades are higher.

  - Low prices on an iPhone or Kindle, when you make your high profit margins from app and book sales.

- It's a product that has little value until a critical mass of people have one (e.g., fax machines).

- You anticipate initial market resistance to your innovative product, so you're pricing low until innovators can spread the word about how great it is. *And* you have add-on products with higher margins for buyers.

Your Assignment

Go ahead and complete the Cost Analysis Worksheet today!

PART 4

Fine-Tuning Your Price

O nce you've picked a ballpark/range for your price (Chapter 7) and calculated your costs (Chapter 8), there's still a lot of work to be done.

Stopping at this point guarantees you are leaving money—probably *a lot* of money—on the table.

Chapter 9 is your last chance to make major changes. It's your opportunity to say, "Wait a minute—this won't be enough profits for me. I want/need more." *And* it will give you the tools to make changes that can transform your offering to something more profitable.

Chapter 10 introduces you to pricing psychology, where a dollar difference—or even a penny (!)—can greatly increase or decrease sales.

CHAPTER 9

Is Your Profit Potential Acceptable?

In-a-Rush Tip

If you're satisfied with your potential profits, as calculated in the previous chapters, you can skip this chapter.

So now that you've established what buyers are prepared to pay (Part 2), and what your costs are (Part 3), how does it look when you subtract your costs from the potential price range?

Are you dancing in the streets over your pending wealth? Great! Then you're almost done. Just some critical fine-tuning to go.

Or did your numbers show low or nonexistent profits? No need to bang your head against a wall or swear. There are

a number of ways you can turn this around, and you're about to see them all in this chapter.

If You're Happy with Your Potential Profits

If you can make a healthy profit given your costs and the price buyers will pay for your combination of benefits, negatives, and price position, you're still not quite finished.

There are enormous differences in buyer demand based upon pricing psychology, which we cover in the next chapter.

You can skip there right now, or read the rest of this chapter to find possible ways to increase your profits even more.

If You're *Not* Happy with Your Potential Profits

Yes, it's disappointing to see low or no profits for an idea you have spent a lot of time developing. But there are still a number of choices available to you.

Best of all, you discovered the problem *before* you spent a bundle launching something that wouldn't be a financial success. When you can either back out of it or change it so that it can be profitable.

Option #1: Dump the Idea and Move On

This chapter will give you a lot of ways to turn your problem into a potential winner. But if you review them and don't find any that would work for your situation, then the best answer is to kill the idea and move on. That's the difference between an entrepreneur who tries a couple of ideas before finding the one that leads to success and a bankrupt entrepreneur without the funds to start his or her next idea: The next one that might actually become a success.

It's really hard for entrepreneurs, given our self-confident makeup, not to think we can be the exception. I do understand because I've been there.

Example: After two successful launches (a magazine and a newsletter), I got test results for a different newsletter that were so-so. Not a terrible failure, but not a success—more like in the "breakeven" area. I was sure I could make it happen because the idea was so good and so needed. (Hint: It was *needed*, but it wasn't *wanted* enough. People don't buy what they need unless they also want it!) So I launched it, and the results were exactly like my tests, despite all my "improvements" that were supposed to make a difference. It lasted three issues, until I cut my losses. Lesson learned? Trust what the market tells you, even if you don't want to.

Not launching a product that can't succeed is not a failure; it's a success. You saved your money. Here are some examples of companies that faced this same choice:

- Porsche AG stopped developing its Porsche 989 when it was discovered the cost would be 30 percent higher than the price that could be achieved in the market.

- Spalding's pump baseball glove was considered a great idea, but a $100 (required) price tag soon put an end to all market chances.

- When Mercedes-Benz introduced its new S-Class in the early 1990s, sales fell significantly short of goals. Analysis revealed that the gap between the customers' requirements and the features offered was too great to achieve the price that had been established (Butscher and Laker, 2000).

Option #2: Change Your Price Positioning

If you can't make enough profits in the price-positioning strategy you chose, can you switch to a higher price positioning? Can you move to competitive instead of penetration? Or can you move to skimming/prestige instead of competitive?

You would obviously have to add benefits or subtract negatives in order to better compete with a higher-priced group of competitors.

Here's how to test out this strategy and see if it will be more profitable for you:

1. Review your worksheets for Chapters 3 and 6.

2. Change the competitors you listed in your Chapter 7 worksheet to a different group of competitors.

3. Look at *their* benefits and negatives, and consider what you would have to change about your product to compete successfully with this new group.

4. Calculate the added costs of those changes and add it to your cost calculations from the Chapter 8 worksheet.

5. Review your new profit potential (new price range – new costs = new profit potential).

How do your potential profits look now? If you are now happy, you can skip to the next chapter for psychological fine-tuning. Or you can continue reading this chapter to find even more ways to increase your profits.

Option #3: Offer Some Higher-Priced Add-Ons

One way to improve your profits is to find options (add-ons) that have a very high profit margin. If enough people buy the add-ons, it raises your overall profit margins.

Explanation: If your basic offering would need to sell for $100, and your total costs are $98, you have just a 2 percent profit margin ($2 profit/$100 price). Suppose you have an add-on that could sell for $10, and your costs are just $1. That's a 90 percent profit margin.

If someone bought both, you'd have sales of $110, with $99 in costs for a 10 percent total profit margin. If half your buyers took the add-on, you'd raise your overall profits from 2 percent to 6 percent.

In some industries, the price of the most basic configuration or basic service is kept artificially low to attract consumers. In those industries, consumers expect to see a certain low price—and if you don't offer that price they will avoid you.

Often in those industries, most consumers don't take just the basic, but they add on additional options—and those add-ons have a higher profit margin.

Go back to your Chapter 3 worksheet and look at all the add-ons that your competitors are offering.

Figure your costs for adding any of them that would be complementary to your product. Then figure out what your potential profits would be on the add-on, given your costs and a price about the same as your competitor(s). That's the easy part.

It's much harder trying to estimate how many buyers would take the add-on instead of the basic version. Short of finding industry data, or talking to retail salespeople (if it's offered in stores), your best chance is talking to people likely to have bought such a product and finding out what they did. This can work especially well if you have a B2B purchase and can attend a trade show or conference where many of the attendees have either purchased or considered such a buy. Beyond any of that, you are left making a guess. In that situation, try to guess conservatively, by underestimating how many people would take it.

Obviously, if you can offer more than one add-on of value to buyers, and all of your add-ons have a fat profit margin, you are in a better position to run without changing your price positioning.

Option #4: Offer Some "Utilities" that Will Allow a Higher Price

Consider the four "utilities" that your product or service provides to buyers. If you can segment customers by their needs for these utilities, you may be able to differentiate your offerings into a basic and a higher-priced version for different groups. This can raise your overall profit margins.

Time Utility

Can you price differently by one of the following?

- Faster service. People will pay a premium for it, unless your competitors already offer it for free.
- Time of day or day of week. People pay more for evening movie tickets, peak-hour electricity, airplane travel during the business week, and late-night taxi rides.
- Seasons. Spring skiing is cheaper than skiing in the winter with more reliable snow. Hotels and travel have "peak season" premiums.

Form Utility

Can your product be offered in different forms? If so, some of those may command premium prices.

- For example, consider soap. The price (and profit margin) is cheapest for bar soap. You get a higher profit margin for liquid soap, perfumed soap, sensitive-skin soap, or soap-on-a-rope.

Place Utility

Can you offer your product or service at a place more convenient to all (or a group of) your potential buyers?

- For example, food delivered to customers' homes, professionals who make house calls or have offices in shopping malls, or exercise professionals who come to businesses for their employees. All these carry a premium price for the buyer convenience.

Possession Utility

If you are in a marketplace where people typically rent (or get limited use of) your type of product or service, is there a group of people willing to pay more to actually own it?

Option #5: Find Customer Segments
Willing to Pay More

There may be sub-groups of targets for whom your service is much more critical than for others. Typically such customer groups will pay more than the others, with some added benefit or feature.

Consider this list of options and evaluate whether or not you could offer an "enhanced" product or service to one or more of these groups:

- Usage segments
  - If all your competitors make "general purpose" products for more than one group, you can raise prices (and profits) by customizing the product for each.
    - For example, you and your competitors make swim goggles used by competitive swimmers and triathletes. If you could customize (even in a small way) so you have Triathlete Swim Goggles and a separate Sprint Swim Goggles (maybe better able to handle diving in the water at the start of the sprint?), you could get higher prices and higher margins.
  - Heavy users versus light. You can save money (less packaging) by making jumbo sizes of your product(s). And you can earn fatter profit margins by making single-person sizes (half the size usually comes at two-thirds or more of the price).
- Psychological segments
  - Can you add a (higher-profit-margin) version that appeals to consumers who want to identify with something?

◆ For example, a credit card with a nursing magazine logo identified the holder as a nurse and was successful.

■ Can you add a "Message" version that appeals to consumers who want to promote a cause?

● Demographic segments

■ Males versus females. Would gender-specific versions sell better? (Hint: Unless it's for young girls, don't just slap pink on it and expect women to prefer it.)

■ Can you add a more advanced (higher profit margin) version for younger consumers? For older?

■ Can you add a "professional" version that has more job-friendly features?

Next Step

If you already show acceptable profits, or you project that one or more ideas from this chapter will allow you to have acceptable profits, you are ready for the next chapter—psychological adjustments to prices.

If none of these ideas will allow you to get an acceptable profit, given your costs and what your analysis of the market shows buyers are willing to pay, you have just two choices left:

1. Kill the product idea and look for something else.

    a. The rationale for this decision was given under "Option 1" in this chapter. You should reread that section.

2. Go ahead and test your product/price combination.

    a. Sometimes there is a benefit or product that produces an unexpectedly large desire in potential buyers. Sometimes the "best wisdom" is wrong.

    b. If you believe strongly in your product and price, you can proceed to Chapters 15 and 16. But do so guardedly.

    c. Understand that you're seeking a long shot. If it comes, great. But don't lose everything on the gamble.

Psychological Adjustments to Your Price

In-a-Rush Tip

Don't skip this critical chapter! But you can skip the "Learn More" at the end.

By reaching this chapter in this book you now have:

- A price range that buyers have shown they will pay for a product of roughly your benefits and your negatives.

- Your costs.

- Knowledge that you can make an acceptable profit given the two points.

Chapter 10 is where you will learn to adjust your prices to take advantage of buyer psychology.

Don't skip this step! Buyers make instinctive judgments about prices based on both constant cultural exposure to numbers and prices and by how our brains are wired. Not paying attention to pricing psychology can cause your product sales to be 10 percent lower, 15 percent, or even worse.

It's that important.

Understanding "Barriers" in Prices

A key part of brain development is learning how to screen out unnecessary "noise" from our senses. Otherwise we would be paralyzed by all the input coming in every minute.

Native speakers of any language that reads left to right, as ours does, have learned that the numbers on the left side of a number are far more important than the numbers on the right. On the right are cents, or dollars. On the left are thousands, millions, or even billions.

In addition to paying more attention to the leftmost parts of numbers, we have also learned that larger equals bigger.

Together these learned perceptions create artificial barriers in how we see numbers. For example, consider your reaction to each of these two prices:

- $1,000

- $999

If you see them together like this, the effect is diluted. Your left (logical) brain can recognize there is only $1 difference between them. But if you saw only one of these prices, attached to something you wanted, your perception of how expensive the item is would be quite different, depending on which of these prices was attached.

That's partially because we've gone from a three-digit number to a four-digit number.

Staying *below* Barriers

Direct-mail and Internet marketers have found that crossing the barrier to a larger leftmost number (e.g., from an "8" to a "9") can cause a drop of 10–15 percent in response.

The largest barriers—with the greatest danger in response fall-off—add an extra digit to the price, as in the above as well as:

- $9.99 to $10.00

- $99 to $100

But you can easily see a 10 percent drop in response by moving from $29 to $30. We're wired to notice the leftmost part of the number. And even though the digits haven't increased, we have moved from a price of $20-something to $30-something.

This isn't evil marketers tricking consumers. Every person over the age of consent in the United States knows that $99 is just one dollar different from $100. So why does it work? Because the $99 price allows consumers to "trick" *themselves.*

Consumers like to feel they are smart shoppers. They like to feel they're getting a deal. Being able to say they paid $90-something for the product makes them feel better than saying they paid "almost $100." In fact, if you asked 100 people (who just spent $99.99 for something) what they paid, I'd be surprised if more than one told you $100. Most will tell you "$99" or "$90-something."

You know—and they know—that $99.99 is virtually the same as $100. But if 10–15 percent fewer customers will buy at $100 as will buy at $99.99, then buyers are telling you something you have to listen to in order to sell. They're telling you to adjust your price so they can both have what they want *and* feel like a smart shopper (or at least not feel like a poor shopper).

Increasing Prices *up to* Barriers

This works the other way as well. It means that prices under the barrier can often be moved up with no drop at all in response, as long as they don't cross a barrier.

Examples:

- Suppose you're considering a price of $9.85. There's a very good chance you could move your price up to $9.95 or $9.99 and not have any drop in response.

- Suppose you're considering $85. You could almost certainly charge $89 and see little if any dropoff.

- I once consulted for a newsletter publisher who was charging $345/year for a subscription. Lots of other not-exactly competitor newsletters were charging $300-something, including $395. Some were charging in the $400-somethings.

- The publisher had neither enough money nor enough subscribers to really test prices, so I told him to just raise the price to $375. I told him I didn't think he'd get any dropoff, and he didn't. So he was pocketing $30 more per subscriber per year with the same number of subscribers.

- This carried some risk, because he passed three smaller barriers, moving from 45 through 55 through 65 up to 75. But my judgment for this industry was that higher $300-something prices were so normal that most companies wouldn't even notice the jump—as long as the leftmost number stayed the same. That would not necessarily be true in a lot of other industries.

Barrier Price Adjustments for You

Your goal in this chapter is to find the three or four best potential prices for your product—all of which are psychologically smart.

Let's say your price range from the Narrowing Your Price Range Worksheet in Chapter 7 is $52–$68. Knowing what you now know about barrier prices, what is one number in that range you absolutely must test? Right below the biggest barrier in your range? Correct. It's $59. So what other prices should you test? The simplest solution is to test the high and the low, so you'd test $52, $59, and $68. However, $68 might not be any different in response from $69, so you might want to test $69 instead of $68.

But it isn't always that clear a choice.

Suppose your ideal price range is $40–$61. Now what do you test? Here's what I'd recommend—based solely on barrier pricing psychology:

- $39,
- $49,
- $59, and
- $62

Let me explain why.

If your ideal range starts with a number right on top of a barrier ($40 in this example), you really need to see how much more you could bring in if you dropped below that barrier. If not $39, then at least $39.99. If you can make an acceptable profit at $40, then you can make an acceptable profit at $39.99 as well. *And* you might have 10–15 percent more units sold!

Why, if your upper number in your range is $61, do I recommend testing $62 instead of $61? Because numbers just over a barrier typically don't do very well. $60 or $61 will usually pull worse than $62. I don't have a proven reason why, but I believe at $60 or $61 you can only compare the price to $60. At $62, you can imagine it being a discount from $70, which would mean the product is both higher quality and a good discount.

Most important: You must pick a price to test that is higher than you believe it is possible to get.

If you don't, you're an idiot. Just like I was an idiot when I didn't test high enough prices for my newsletter launch—which resulted in my missing out on $38,000 in profits I could have pocketed.

Be sure to test the high price of your range. And if that high price ends in a 0 or a 1 (as in $60 or $61), make sure to move up to $62 or $64.

Numbers that Say "Discount" to Buyers

There are certain numbers you can use that cause buyers to think your product or service is discounted. And that can be a good thing—or a bad thing—depending on the perceptions you want for your offering.

Pennies in any price over $40 look like a discount price, which buyers in most industries will perceive as meaning the *product* is a discount-type of product.

The only industry where I have noticed prices like $999.99 on high-quality products is in the consumer electronics industry. In almost all other industries, a price of $999.99 would signal a lower-quality product than one priced at $995.

A "9" on the far right end of a product/service price also signals "discount" to buyers, often with the "discount" label extending to the product's quality.

Examples:

- The consumer health newsletter industry has a lot of offerings at $19.99, $29.99, and $39.99. Harvard Medical School publishes a number of consumer health newsletters. Their prices are $22, $24, and $28. See how much classier their image is—just from not ending in a "9" or having pennies in their prices?

- High-end restaurants predominantly use a "0" or a "5" as the farthest-right digit of their menu prices, while low-end fast-food restaurants primarily use a "9." In a number of studies, Naipaul and Parsa (2001) found consumer reaction to menus from fictitious restaurants could be influenced by the rightmost digit of the prices. Subjects rated menus with prices ending in a "0" as higher in quality than those with menu prices ending in a "9."

Another reason I advise against having pennies in any price over $40 for any product other than those with a penetration price positioning is that it makes the price look longer. Remember from "barrier pricing" previously that the longer the number, the bigger we perceive it.

Test Your Knowledge!

Pick the best price examples:

- $22.99 versus $24 for a prestige product
    - $24 reinforces your prestige positioning and will likely do better or equal to $22.99.

- $20.95 versus $22.95 for a competitive product
    - Prices just above a barrier number ($20) are likely to do less well than prices farther above. It's likely that $22.95 will pull more or at least the same number of orders.

- $52.99 versus $53
    - Because of the pennies, $52.99 looks bigger and may draw fewer orders than $53.
    - The only instance where I would recommend the $52.99 price here is where you're trying hard to be perceived as the biggest discounter in the industry. If having the lowest price is your positioning, then go with the pennies.

- $19.99 versus $20

  - This is a trick choice. The pennies may cause you to believe $19.99 would be perceived bigger, but this crosses a barrier where the leftmost number changes (from a "1" to a "2"). In this case the barrier crossing is more important than the pennies. $20 would probably pull 5–10 percent worse.

Visually Appealing Prices

If you have a shockingly low price, you want it to stand out dramatically. You'll put it in larger type and bold. You'll feature it.

Any other price should not stand out. You want it to go down smoothly, like syrup—mildly pleasing, nothing shocking, nothing that causes the swallower to react with a frown or (worst of all!) choking.

For example, there is research on using a "7" in your prices; typically it can raise response rates. If you look at most magazine and newsletter subscription prices you'll see most of them end in a "7" or at least include a "7." That's because publications do a lot of price testing and they have found buyer preference for a "7" to be a fact. (You can see specific research on this in my *Pricing Psychology Report* book at PricingPsychology.com.)

Some people knowing this have taken it to extremes. They figure if one "7" is great, then more "7s" would be even better.

Yet suppose you were considering products with the following prices:

- $7.77, or

- $777

Seeing prices like these is likely to stop you in your tracks and make you focus on the price. You might even frown in puzzlement. Both of these are very bad responses to elicit from your potential buyers.

I recently did pricing for an online startup where the prices varied by frequency, so you had a table display. The client had read my *Pricing Psychology Report* and wondered why I didn't have "7s" in all the prices. I've created phony charts here to show you what I mean, without showing you the client's actual prices or categories. Consider your reaction if you saw a pricing table like one of the two in Exhibit 10.1.

Example A looks like what you'd expect to see. Example B will likely cause you to take a second look at the prices and wonder what is going on with all the "7s." It's not what you'd normally see, so you'll wonder about it.

Buyers wondering about your prices is a bad thing. Something this unusual will cause many of your buyers to

EXHIBIT 10.1 PERCEPTIONS OF MULTIPLE-PRICE CHARTS		
EXAMPLE A		
Per-Week Advertising Prices		
1–4 Weeks	**5–12 Weeks**	**13–22 Weeks**
Banner on home page $85	$75	$65
Banner on category home page $75	$65	$55
Banner on other pages $65	$55	$45
EXAMPLE B		
Per-Week Advertising Prices		
1–4 Weeks	**5–12 Weeks**	**13–22 Weeks**
Banner on home page $87	$77	$67
Banner on category home page $77	$67	$57
Banner on other pages $67	$57	$47

wonder if you're trying to "game" them. If they even consider that, your pricing strategy has failed.

People who think pricing is unfair have been known to refuse to buy something they really wanted just because of it. These same people get angry enough to tell others. For a great book on this topic, check out *The Price Is Wrong* by Sarah Maxwell.

Moral of the story: Don't make your prices look "strange."

Selling to Businesses

All this price psychology applies to B2B (selling to businesses) as well as B2C (selling to consumers). After all, businesses are managed by people, and all people want to feel like smart buyers.

Let's say you're pricing a consulting service, and you feel the correct market price is somewhere around $20,000. Let's look at some possible prices you could charge:

- $20,000
  - Two problems with this number: It moves the left number from 1 to 2, and it's right on top of the barrier. (See the earlier "Barrier Price Adjustments for You" section.)
- $19,999

- ■ The problem with this number is it sounds like a discount shop—where the buyer is risking low-quality work.

- ● $19,750

  - ■ This is the number I would recommend. It's below a big barrier, doesn't have the "99" discount taint, *and* it includes a "7." (See the "Visually Appealing Prices" section.)

- ● $22,275

  - ■ This is another price to consider. If the last time you quoted a price, you got the job without much discussion about the price, then you are underpriced. This is a good price to quote because it is not on top of a barrier, and it looks like you're not rounding up to gouge someone. And it has a "7."

Learn More about Thresholds

Every human sense has limits. An absolute threshold marks the divider between response and no response. For example, the absolute threshold of sound humans can hear differs from that for dogs. JND stands for "just noticeable difference" and refers to our ability (or lack of one) to differentiate between small changes.

For example, a computer putting out a specific frequency note can go up or down in tone a few steps before it is noticeable to the human ear. So research focuses on how much of a change is required before it is "noticeable."

This research most often informs product-size decisions. Here's an example:

Suppose you make M&Ms–type candy, and your biggest selling package sells for $.99 for 2 ounces. You have tested and tested higher prices, but sales take a nosedive when you go to $1.00 or more. Yet your costs have gone up and your CEO is demanding you stop the drop in profits.

What do you do? You could reduce the ounces of candy in the bag. But, using the insights gained from JND threshold research, you want to make the reduction not noticeable. You will list the correct (lower) ounces on the new bag, but you're hoping someone who picks up a new bag won't suddenly look at it and think it feels light. It takes some testing. What's the correct weight? 1.9 ounces? 1.8? The yogurt industry has used this tactic, shrinking individual containers substantially.

But at some point this will no longer work. After all, a 2-ounce yogurt would be ridiculous, as would a fingernail-sized candy bar.

Suppose you don't believe you can go any smaller in what you offer. Your only way to increase profits at that point is to raise the price—and offer a bigger bag. But here you want JND to work the opposite direction. You want to give enough more product in the bag that consumers *will* *notice* the change (but add no more than needed!).

So, in this situation, you might raise your price to $1.25, add as many candies to the bag as needed for it to be noticeable, and have an "X% more!" or other message on the bag itself to be *sure* it's noticed.

Threshold research also suggests that there are price points both too high and too low to be acceptable to consumers (e.g., Fouilhe, 1970; Monroe, 1971a).

Gabor and Granger (1966) found absolute price thresholds, high and low, for five common products. They also found evidence suggesting low prices were perceived more negatively to high-income groups than high prices were perceived negatively to low-income groups.

Zaichkowsky (1985) showed that high-product-involvement consumers are less likely to risk a low-priced option.

Learn More about the Effect of Numbers

There is some odd research in psychology about the ability of random numbers to change what people say they will pay in prices. It's the "anchoring and adjusting" aspect of prospect theory first identified by Tversky and Kahneman (1974).

They found that a number derived from spinning a wheel would nevertheless serve as an anchor when subjects were asked for a number for something completely different. Others also found this.

Ariely, Loewenstein, and Prelec (2003) replicated this type of study by showing students six products, with no indication as to price. (The products each had a retail value of about $70.) Students were then asked if they would buy each for the last two digits of their social security numbers, translated into dollars. After giving an accept or reject response to each, students were then asked to state the highest price they would be willing to pay for each. The impact of the social security numbers on the subsequent price students were willing to pay was significant for all six products. In fact, those subjects with the highest last two digits were willing to pay three times what subjects with the lowest two digits would pay.

Additional experiments by the authors demonstrate what they call "coherent arbitrariness." They show that consumers respond appropriately to price changes that are called to their attention (coherent), but their initial anchors can be arbitrarily derived from exposure to meaningless numbers.

Wansink, Kent, and Hoch (1998) used this theory to explain consumer purchases of multiple units, where the price of a single unit is the anchor. They found that usage of a high anchor (e.g., "Limit 12 to a Person") can increase purchase quantities even where there is no discount given for the additional purchases.

PART 5

Testing Your Prices

Developing the optimal price requires testing. Period. Too many clients want me to pick their prices, so they can publish them and get back to business. No consultant can give you *the* best price. We can only give you a *few* best prices. You need to test those few prices in order to pick the best.

The differences can be astronomical in profits!

In Chapters 11 and 12, we'll look at how you test prices, what prices to test, and how to test for no cash outlay (or at least very little).

Believe me, I understand the urge to just get on with it. You've done all the work thus far, done the spreadsheets, gotten excited about the price you now have—and need to get back to the 1,000 other things you've back-burnered while doing this.

Don't stop now. Testing can mean thousands to millions in profits for you. And it can be done relatively quickly. Read on!

CHAPTER 11

Testing Prices

When you reach this chapter you should now know:

- Prices buyers are proven willing to pay for a product with your positioning and your benefits and negatives
- Your costs
- That you can earn an acceptable (hopefully great!) profit given the prior two points
- That you have considered buyer psychology in setting the actual numbers
- That you now have three to four very good prices from which to choose

What you *don't* know, however, is that you are at a dangerous point in determining prices. A point where you could lose *a lot* of money! See the next section.

The Psychology of *You*—in Setting Prices

The problem is, you already have a strong feeling that one of your three or four prices is best. Am I correct? And you're feeling this very strong urge to just run with that price.

There is too much money at stake for you to give in to that urge. You need to "test-drive" your three or four choices and let buyers tell you which one is best.

People buy for a lot of reasons, most of them focused on the product. Often the price is a very minor consideration. If you don't test prices, you will blame any poor performance in sales on your price—when it very likely won't be that at all. So you'll waste a lot of time spinning pricing wheels when you may need to adjust part of your *product*.

Example:

- Suppose you set a price of $75 for your new product. And sales come in at about one-third of what you expected. If you haven't previously tested prices that were lower, your gut reaction will be to lower prices—when that might not be the problem at all.

- This very thing happened to me on a product where I had foolishly *not* tested prices. So I lowered it to a price test of $65 and $67. But neither of those lower prices changed anything. Meanwhile, I was throwing away $8–10 profit from each sale at the lower price while I found out the price is not the issue.

- This also delayed my recognition that the real problem was the marketing message. Once I rewrote the web site material, sales moved up to 80 percent of what I had originally expected. And that's where they're staying.

  - Price was *not* a problem.

- Marketing copy *was* a problem.

- My sales expectations *were also* a problem—which can be expected when launching a completely new product!

A second psychological problem in people who set prices is a tendency to set too low a price. This is especially true in people selling services, such as consultants, freelance writers, designers, etc.

I bring this up because without testing prices, you are more likely to pick too low a price than too high a price. One of the best pieces of wisdom I gained from attending a newsletter publisher conference was this:

> You are most likely to *over*estimate how many subscribers (buyers) you will attract, but to *under*estimate the price buyers will pay.

I have found this to be true in other industries as well. In fact, once I look at a company's business or marketing plan, I almost always suggest lowering its estimates of buyers, as well as recommending a number of ways to bring in higher prices.

There is very little academic research on testing prices both higher and lower than the one calculated to be ideal. Among practitioners, testing both higher and lower prices is accepted wisdom. It would be hard to find an experienced direct response marketer who has not been surprised by a winning price that differed substantially from expectations. Examples:

- In 2005 I tested $37 and $47 for an e-book originally offered at $27. Despite the book being just 52 pages in length, the $47 price produced just 1.5 percent fewer buyers than $27—and a lot more profits!

- A test of the same three prices for a different e-book in a different marketplace—with over 100 pages—found $37 the most profitable price.

Can You Test?

The best, cheapest (usually free!) way to test prices is online. Unfortunately, some business simply cannot test online. They include:

- Consultants (unless you do 100+ of a single type of consulting job in a year)
- Custom manufacturers
- Bars and restaurants
- Hair salons and barber shops
- Sellers of very expensive equipment to businesses
- Sellers of anything where prices are traditionally negotiated

If You Cannot Test Prices

If you cannot sell your product online—even for a test—and/or cannot sell at least 100 units in two to three months, then you are stuck making your best guess from the three or four prices you previously identified.

My recommendation is to pick a price higher than the one you think best. I recommend this because of these reasons:

- It is easier to drop prices if you don't see enough sales than it is to increase prices if sales are coming fast and easy.

- Even if you are determined to launch at one price, you can always set your price at the next higher number, then give an "introductory" discount down to the price you strongly think is best. This gives you two big benefits:

  - If sales come very easy, you can eliminate the discount at the end of the period and see if sales continue strong.

  - Your "sale" gives an incentive to buy that should boost sales higher than you would have seen without it.

The Difference between Testing and Research

While you will see many different definitions and distinctions between these two, the easiest for me is that testing requires you to actually try to *sell* your product or service. Research does not require this.

The last thing you want when you're setting a price is research giving you people's opinions about the right price. And there's a lot of bad pricing research out there that does just that.

You've probably seen research that asks "What's the highest price you would reasonably expect to pay for X?" The answer to this research is worthless—even if it's put into charts and a professional-looking presentation.

Here's why pricing research that asks for opinions is worthless:

1. People don't really know—until they're faced with something they want to buy and a price for that something.
2. People will lie—figuring they're doing a service to themselves and other buyers by helping keep prices low.
3. People don't really care; they're just trying to get through the survey so they can go do something they will enjoy instead of answering meaningless questions.

Pricing research that is choice-based conjoint, which requires the respondent to select from different combinations of product or service and price, is the best we can do in pricing research.

Price testing, however, is pure gold. No questions for people to answer. Just an offering and a price. No questions on the results, either. You add up the number of buyers at each price and your total profits—and you have a clear and (assuming you follow the instructions in the next chapter!) reliable answer.

CHAPTER 12

Using Google to Test Prices for Free (or Almost Free)

In-a-Rush Tip

Don't skip this critical chapter!

However, if you already have a Google AdWords account, you can skip steps 1–3 under "A/B Split Testing with Google AdWords."

Two Methods for Almost-Free Testing!

You may not have to spend a cent to test prices. For this you can thank Google, a company that has done many wonderful things particularly for small businesses, but that now strides industries like Godzilla, squashing a few thousand people here and there as it passes by. If I was creating a slang dictionary, I'd list Google first under "love-hate relationship."

Google has two different ways you can test prices:

1. **A/B split testing** (Note: You can test more than two choices, so A/B split testing can actually be A/B/C or A/B/C/D split testing.)

2. **Google Optimizer** (This is a form of multivariate testing, which used to require buying an expensive

software package, or an even more expensive testing service. Now, thanks to Google, it is free to you.)

The advantage of A/B split testing is that it is easiest to set up; you won't need help from a web designer.

The disadvantage of A/B split testing—and why you would instead use Google Optimizer—is that A/B split testing can only test one thing (e.g., prices *or* headlines) at a time. With Google Optimizer, you can test multiple items at the same time. But you might need webmaster help in setting up the test.

A/B Split Testing with Google AdWords

For a couple hundred bucks spent in search advertising on Google AdWords, you can easily and quickly find the answer to one—and only one—marketing question.

- It might be price: Which of these three prices should I run with?

- It might be ad headlines: Which of these three headlines will pull best?

If you have not done search engine marketing before, don't worry about how much you will spend. You will be able to limit the total amount you spend each day to whatever number you desire. If you set the cutoff at $20/day, then

if enough people click on your ad that you've run up $20 in charges, Google stops running the ad for the rest of the day, and starts it back the next day. And you can change this number at any time.

Following are the steps you need to take in order to test prices using Google AdWords and an A/B split.

If you already have a Google AdWords account, or already know how to set one up, you can skip steps 1–3.

1. Go to Google.com. Under the search box, you will see a link for "Advertising Programs." Click on it, then click on the "Sign Up Now" button under "Google AdWords" (*not* AdSense!).

2. Allow yourself to just bumble along and figure it out as you go. Google guides you by the hand pretty well, and has lots of "Help" options, including a phone number if you really run into trouble. (You probably won't need the phone number.) Notes:

   a. You can work on this for days (or months) without it costing you a cent. Just click the "No thanks, I'll set up billing later" whenever it asks.

   b. Only when you're completely done and ready to run ads should you go to the billing tab. At that point Google will charge you $5 for the setup and start running your ads.

3. You'll set up a "campaign" for which you design an ad (go ahead and do a rough one—you can edit it later) and pick appropriate keywords. You'll also link to the web page where you're offering your product for sale.

4. Warning: Google wants you to let *it* determine how much you should bid for an ad. This is like asking a fox to guard your hen house. Only if you have money to throw away should you do this! What you want to avoid is "automatic bidding." You instead want "manual bidding."

   a. Click on the "Campaigns" tab. If you have more than one Campaign, you must do this separately for each campaign.

   b. Click on the "Settings" tab.

   c. Scroll down to "Bidding and Budget," then look at "Bidding Option." It should say "manual" and not "automatic." If it says automatic, change it!

5. Scroll further down to "Advanced Settings" then to "Ad Rotation."

6. Set Ad Rotation to this choice: "Rotate—show ads more evenly." This option is necessary to do split testing. Otherwise, Google will start giving preference to one of your test ads over the others, which will risk the validity of your results.

7. Make as many copies of your web landing page (where you sell your product) as you have prices to test. Three prices? Then make three copies of your page, each with a different URL. For example:

   a. YourCompany.com/new1.htm

   b. YourCompany.com/new2.htm

   c. YourCompany.com/new3.htm

   Notes:

   i. Don't do something this obvious, or knowledgeable people seeing "new2" will search for "new" with other numbers to see if they can find a better price.

   ii. Make sure they are all different from the page someone would go to if they clicked on a link to your home page. Your home page (or landing page people would find by going to your web site) must be separate from your three price test pages.

   iii. Your home or "normal" landing page should carry your highest test price for the duration of the test. That's because people seeing a test page might also go to your home page and find the offer there. Nobody minds having found a cheaper price offer. But online customers *really* resent (wouldn't you?) finding their special offer is more expensive than the standard offer on your web site.

8. Make sure each of the three test pages is exactly the same—except for the price. Set up one test page for each of the prices you want to test. And set up your fulfillment/accounting system so that each test page gets billed for the correct amount and the product or service is provided. Make sure your accounting system can separately track sales from the highest price test page and from the non-test home or landing page (which should also have the highest price). As long as it can identify the source page of the order, you will be fine.

9. In your Google AdWords account, go to the rough ad you set up (under the tab "Ads"). If you put your cursor over it, a little pencil icon will appear. Click on that to edit your ad.

10. Revise and polish it until you think it will work great for people who are searching for the keywords you selected.

11. Notice the two locations at the bottom for your URL. The first one is the one that will show to searchers. Make it a direct link to your home page (which carries your highest test price). Example: YourCompany.com/

NewBrandName. People will only go to that page if they type in your URL. Tips:

a. Don't put in "www." It takes up space and makes the URL harder to read and look longer to type in.

b. Make sure to capitalize the start of each word in your URL (see the example in step 11) so it is easier to read.

c. Note that some number of people will not click on your ad, but will type in the URL that shows. You want them to *not* go to one of your test pages, because it could hurt your test reliability.

   i. Because some will want to type in your URL, this shown URL should be as short and easy as you can make it.

12. At the second URL line, type in the URL for one of your price test pages (e.g., YourCompany.com/wiehelsiee or whatever you name one of your three test pages. Note that this can be a long URL because it will not be seen by anyone. It just designates where the person who clicks on that ad will be taken.

13. Click on "New Ad" then "Text Ad" to set up your second new ad. It should be *exactly the same* as your first ad, except for the bottom line with your web site test page location.

14. Set up as many ads as you have price tests, each pointing to one of the test pages. It's important that all the ads look exactly the same to the potential buyer. The only difference should be the page they're sent to.

15. Give Google your credit card number and go live.

a. Your accounting system will tell you how many sales you had from each of the test pages.

b. The "Ads" tab in your Google AdWords campaign will tell you how many people clicked on each of your three ads.

c. You should run the test until you get *at least* 40 orders at your most successful price. Run it until you get 75 orders if you can. That said, I know people who have made decisions based on fewer orders. But having under 40 responses raises the risk that your results are not reliable.

d. From the AdWords data Google provides, you will learn:

i. What percentage of those who clicked on each ad went on to actually buy from you. For example:

- What percentage bought at price A?

- What percentage bought at price B?

- What percentage bought at price C?

ii. The total dollars you earn (revenues) for each of the prices. For example:

- number of buyers at price A times price A

- number of buyers at price B times price B

- number of buyers at price C times price C

iii. How much profit you made from each, after subtracting your product costs.

iv. Your Google costs should be roughly the same because Google should be showing each ad about the same number of times. So you don't need to calculate that into your price tests.

Using Google Optimizer to Test Multiple Things

Google Optimizer brings high level research tools (multivariate testing) to the average person and business. Specifically, it allows you to test multiple things at the same time (e.g., prices, headlines, photos, etc.).

This is especially valuable for new products and services because:

- You have so many things needing testing.

- You probably don't have much traffic to your web site yet. If you were to test headlines, prices, and calls-to-action with A/B split testing, you would be running tests for a long time in order to get enough sales for the results to be statistically valid. With Google Optimizer, you can get all that information in just one test—thus much quicker. And the quicker you can start running your most profitable prices, headlines, etc., the quicker you'll earn the most profits.

Google's Website Optimizer is a free tool. You won't need to buy search engine ads—*if* you already have a lot of traffic coming to your site. Otherwise, you will have to do something to drive traffic to your pages in order to run a successful price test. Translation: You may need to buy AdWords to bring in the traffic for the test.

Again, Google has great help for you in setting up and using the program. One problem is the complexity of the setup. Under the FAQs, here's what Google says about needing a webmaster:

Q. "Will I need help from my webmaster?"

A. "If you don't know HTML, or you don't have access to edit the HTML source of your website, you'll need some technical help to use Website Optimizer. Specifically, you might need technical help obtaining the original HTML content of your site and installing the experiment code on your site. Don't worry—we provide in-depth instructions that will guide you or your webmaster through any technical portions of the experiment set-up."[1]

A complete overview of the program can be found at www.google.com/support/websiteoptimizer/bin/answer.py?answer=61144. In case this link no longer works when you read this, just search Google for "Website Optimizer Installation Guide—Multivariate."

How to Get Started

There are a few steps to take in order to get started (before you even talk to your webmaster):

1. Understand the limitations of Google's Website Optimizer. The most important is that it cannot test items that move around on your web page.

Examples:

a. You can test different prices, but they all have to be listed in the same place on the page. You cannot have one price at the top of the page tested against a price near the bottom of the page. Same with headlines—all the tests have to have the headlines in the same position on the page.

---

[1]Google Website Optimizer FAQs.

b. While you would normally keep headlines and prices in one location, this also means you can't test different photos—or the same photo—in different locations on the page.

2. Decide what you want to test.

   a. List the specific prices you wish to test.

   b. List the specific headlines you wish to test.

   c. Other possible things to test are photos, terms of the offer, guarantees. These are the additional things most likely to have an impact on your sales—*after* price and headlines.

3. Decide who's going to do it for you:

   a. Your webmaster. If so, e-mail the overview of the program link given previously and get a price from him or her.

   b. Google has a list of "Authorized Website Optimizer Consultants" you can pay to do it for you. This is not as good, because it is a new person given access to your web site. If you don't have a regular webmaster, it may well be worth it. Get a price from three or four of them.

   c. You have two choices for doing it yourself:

      i. Do it all yourself, if you are comfortable working with the HTML on your site.

      ii. Do it mostly yourself, up to adding the HTML Google generates. At that point, bring in your webmaster.

4. You can reach Google's Website Optimizer by going to www.google.com/websiteoptimizer.

5. From there, click on the "Start Testing Now" button.

6. From this page, you can either create a new account, or sign in with another Google account you have, including AdWords. (Note, however, that these are two separate programs.)

7. Once past this page you can access all Google help and FAQs if you run into trouble. There are also suggestions on setting up reliable tests.

Regrets!

Once you've set up and run your first test, you will be very upset with yourself that you weren't doing it sooner.

I'm constantly telling my students that marketers don't have to be rocket scientists. And there's no reason to leave making profits to chance.

Smart pricers let the customer tell them (through their purchase behavior, *not* through their opinions) what they want and what they're willing to pay.

The skill required in pricing is coming up with the best prices to test. That's what this book helps you develop. The final step is seeing—through testing—exactly which of those prices will give you the most profits.

Once you have your answers, plan more testing to see if you can't find prices/terms/offers that would be even *more* profitable.

PART 6

Pricing in Special Situations

Some pricing situations are unique enough that they introduce different problems and opportunities.

Chapter 13 looks more specifically at pricing service businesses.

Chapters 14 and 15 look at pricing new-to-the-market products/services. New products face more challenges—mostly due to established competitors.

Chapter 16 looks at working with discounts.

This Part is different. My goal in this book is to provide you with both the knowledge you need to set prices profitably and to provide *quick* help for those with little time.

The chapters in this section are like an extended "Learn More" section that you've seen in other chapters.

You don't need these chapters to set profitable prices!

However, if you can spare the time, these chapters can give you additional ideas for your specific situation. Ideas you can test to develop even *more* profitable prices.

In these chapters, you'll get a lot of research on prices and how consumers view them and respond to them. Doing research on pricing is one of my favorite activities. It's great to come up with questions—and then be able to go find answers.

Yes, the writing in these four chapters is much more dense. It's for those looking to advance from the ability to set more profitable pricing than most, to setting the most profitable prices possible.

I find insights on pricing and consumer behavior fascinating. I hope you will too.

Or . . . you can skip this section and consider your pricing "done"!

CHAPTER 13

Pricing Services

In-a-Rush Tip

You can skip this chapter if you sell products, not services.

Also, you can skip chapters 13 through 16 if you need to set prices immediately. These chapters give you additional ideas to test down the road, to continue improving the profitability of your pricing.

Imagine No Chapter 13!

I wanted to skip Chapter 13, but my book editors overruled me. Why skip it? To help sensitize you to the power of numbers. You see that power when:

- High-rise buildings in the United States skip a 13th floor and go right from 12 to 14, because otherwise they would have to discount the rentals they get on that floor.

- People in Japan avoid elective surgery on the 4th of any month ("shi" is the number 4 and also means death in Japanese).

- More people buy products with a "7" in the price.

- Many more people will buy a product at $99.99 than at $100.

I recommend you reread Chapter 10 and start profiting from a smarter use of numbers in your pricing strategy.

The Complications of Setting Prices for Services

Many problems complicate the problem of selling services. A few of them are:

- Pricing by the hour versus the job

- Finding out what your competitors charge

- Comparing your services to a competitors—when what you're offering depends somewhat (or a lot!) on the person providing the service

Additional problems arise when the service business is a sole proprietorship (as are most):

- Pricing when you're desperate for work (or at least when you have more available time than work)

- Pricing when your variable costs are almost zero

The Myth of Pricing Based on "What You Want to Earn"

Almost all articles on pricing services at some point will tell you to price based on what you want to earn. For example, say you want to earn $60,000 a year before taxes, and you're willing to work 40 hours a week, 30 of which you think will be productive (earning) time. You factor in two weeks of sick days and three weeks of vacation. That means you'll need to charge $42.55 per hour.

Sounds very scientific, doesn't it? But here's the problem: Why would I want to earn $60,000? If the choice is mine, why wouldn't I want $80,000? $100,000? Heck, if I'm honest, I want to earn $10,000,000 each year. Wouldn't you?

When you're pricing services, the question is *not* what you want to earn—but what the market will pay.

And here the pricing gets even more complicated.

- It's much easier to say what a pair of shoes is worth than what a good time is worth.

- Buyers have an idea what a meal is worth because they've purchased the ingredients. They've also eaten in restaurants.

- Buyers have no idea what your specific consulting services are worth.

- If a picture is worth a thousand words, what's a photographer worth in cold, hard cash?

Pricing by the Hour versus the Job

This problem comes from two opposing desires:

- Service providers want to charge by the hour because:

  - It's easier to calculate.

  - They don't have to worry about extra demands from a client abusing their time.

- Clients want to pay by the job because:

    - It's easier to budget for.

    - They don't have to worry about service providers running up hours to squeeze more money out of them.

What's to be done?

The simple answer is to do what your competitors do, if they are uniform.

- If all writers price by the hour (or the word), then you can, too (and may have to in order to sell your services).

- If all accountants in your area price by the hour, you can, too (and may have to in order to compete).

If your competitors differ—or if you want to see if pricing differently can be a competitive benefit—then I recommend you test what is most profitable for you in terms of both landing customers and profitability on those customers.

Offer the next several potential customers the option. Give them a price per hour and a fixed price for the job. See what they take. My suspicion is a large percentage will take the fixed job.

If customers prefer it and your competitors don't offer it, this could be an advantage for you.

How to Protect Yourself from Client Add-Ons to a Fixed Price Job

If you create job proposals, there's a clear way to protect yourself. Write your proposal for each project in great detail, showing exactly what you will do and what you need from the client. I typically do a two- or three-page proposal for potential consulting jobs (single-spaced with lots of detail).

In addition to preventing no-cost add-ons that aren't in the proposal, this tactic has many other advantages:

- In spelling out the job in detail, you better understand yourself exactly what is entailed and how many hours roughly it will take. That makes your price better in tune with the work it will require.

- The detail impresses the potential client in several ways:

    - It shows them you are organized and thorough.

    - It shows them the *huge* amount of work required—in case they were considering just piling it onto an employee.

    - It shows them where what you're doing requires skills none of their employees have.

    - If possible, it also shows skills required that few if any of your competitors have.

- It gives them a feeling of partnership in the project, because at the end you give a price based on the above detail and ask for anything they would want to add to the project or could subtract from it. If so, that will often lead to a revised price.

- Psychologically, it makes your price seem lower or more reasonable when it is listed after all the work you'll be doing to earn it.

Finding What Service Competitors Charge

This is not a problem for service businesses where prices are posted. Unfortunately, much service pricing is not posted.

Knowing what your competitors charge is critical for successful pricing, so you may have to get creative. Here are some possibilities when prices are not posted:

1. Ask the price.

You may be able to walk into establishments or e-mail online service businesses and ask their price.

2. Ask your salespeople the price.

Salespeople often have competitive information that somehow never makes it to management. If you employ salespeople, make getting competitor price information part of their jobs.

3. Have someone else ask the price.

   a. If you are known to local establishments, you may need to have a friend or relative walk in and ask.

   b. If you're trying to find out competitor prices of accountants, lawyers, etc., you may need a business friend who can ask about their services and prices.

4. Ask your (indirect) competitors their prices.

   a. This gets a little tricky, because competitors talking about their prices is illegal! And nobody except a good friend (and maybe not even a good friend) is willing to talk actual price. But you can ask something like this: "I'm trying to price a service where I (short description) but I have no idea what others are charging. Do you have some idea of the *range* of prices others might be charging?"

   b. Notice that by not asking what he or she is charging, you make it easier for the person to feel comfortable giving you a number. (It will probably be what the person is charging—but you can both pretend it isn't.)

     ■ Make sure you ask this of at least three people, to protect yourself from one person answering unreasonably high or low just to see you fail!

5. Buy from your competitors.

   a. If need be, you can buy from competitors. For example, if a spa or salon doesn't list all its prices, you (or a friend) could go in and buy a treatment, then ask for prices for everything else offered.

b. If it isn't too expensive, buying from your competitors is a very good thing. You can see:

    i. Exactly how good a service they provide and where they are lacking

    ii. If particular employees are good or bad

    iii. How the business is run

    iv. The atmosphere they create

    v. Anything unusual they do that you wouldn't have thought up yourself

6. Ask your potential client.

When your potential client is a business, you can ask: "Do you have a range of what you're willing to spend on this project? So I don't give you a proposal for something beyond your budget." I have almost always received a thoughtful answer to this question.

Picking Your Price Positioning

Once you know what some of your competitors charge, you can better assess the proper price positioning strategy to take. If competitors better than you charge X, you're going to need to charge X minus something, unless you can improve what you offer. If your competitors have lower attributes (credentials, features, glamour, etc.), then you'll want to price higher.

An interesting research study was done to answer the question of how much more (or less) expensive than competitors a service should be. Arnold, Hoffman, and McCormick (1989) looked at four differentiators of the service, including:

- Availability (How available are other options?)

- Testability (Can your results be proven? Can they be partially tried?)

- Commitment (What's required of the buyer in dollars or in time?)

- Price sensitivity (How price sensitive are potential buyers as a group?)

The authors concluded that services can command more premium prices the more the services are unavailable to the consumer and the more they can be tested.

They further conclude that price sensitivity is a guiding factor for the amount of customization versus standardization you offer for the service.

What Your Price Says about Your Firm

Part of the impact of a price position in a competitive environment is in its effect on buyer perceptions of quality.

A correlation between higher fees and perceived higher quality was found (Anonymous, 2003) for accounting services, which are high in credence attributes (those attributes difficult to evaluate even after the service has been performed).

The author concluded that in high-risk scenarios, people prefer those professionals who charge higher fees.

Ask yourself if you were on trial *for your life*, which of the following attorneys you'd want to hire—based solely on their prices:

- $390/hour
- $350/hour
- $325/hour
- $250/hour

I submit that given any way you could afford it (and even if you couldn't!) you would not want to hire the $250/hour attorney.

Suppose you have decided to have a face lift. You've checked out local doctors and found four who do the procedure and who have no complaints against them. Their prices are:

- $15,000
- $14,000
- $13,000
- $9,000

Be honest. You wouldn't want to hire the $9,000 doctor, would you?

This rejection of a lowest-priced alternative happens when the risks of bad performance are very high.

Let's instead consider an amusement park. If we have two choices that sound about the same and one is substantially lower, many of us (probably most) would take the cheaper alternative. There's no risk to a bad choice. If we don't like it, we can go to the other one another day.

However, consider the same scenario if you're a young man picking the amusement park to which to take a date who is important to you. In that case, the higher-priced option would provide some psychological protection against the risk of a bad experience that might influence the date.

Of course, the risk of a bad criminal attorney, a bad tax advisor, or a bad plastic surgeon is exponentially greater.

Rejection of the lowest price alternative also happens where we don't have enough other ways of ascertaining quality than the price.

How to Charge Higher Prices to Those Willing to Pay More

Many, many services can be more profitable by charging higher prices to those willing to pay extra and lower prices to those who are the most price sensitive.

How can you discover who among your customers doesn't really care if your price is higher? You don't have to figure this out. You can structure your pricing so your customers divide *themselves* into groups based on their price sensitivity.

These technique works well for movie theaters, sports parks, amusement parks, and many other services.

Look at your business and find the most popular:

- Time of day for purchasing
- Days of the week
- Turnaround time
- Anything else where customers prefer something specific

Then, price your services higher for those most desired scenarios, and offer lower prices for the least desired. Examples include:

- Bargain matinee rates for theaters and films
- Bargain weekday morning prices for amusement parks
- Bargain services with a three-day turnaround

Just remember: You're not charging extra for peak times. Instead, you're offering bargain rates for un-peak times. Psychologically it's a huge difference. Nobody wants to pay an "add-on" fee. But people love having ways to get a discount.

Note

In several industries, people are used to paying an add-on for a "rush" job. That doesn't mean they like it. Ask yourself how many people are paying for your rush work. If not many, consider making your rush price your "regular" price and your rush delivery timeframe also "regular," then offering x percent discount if customers are willing to take slower (two-day? three-day?) delivery. You could get a lot more people paying higher prices. (Just make sure you could handle them with your quicker service!)

This way, those who really don't care about your prices can come/buy when they want. Those who are price sensitive can feel good about changing their behavior in order to get a deal.

It's a win/win situation for all concerned—including your profits!

CHAPTER 14

Pricing New Products/Services, Part 1

When Your Brand Is Unknown

In-a-Rush Tip

You can skip this chapter if you're re-pricing an established product.

Save it for when you next have to price a new product or service. It contains a lot of research that can help, but that will slow you down if you need a price this afternoon!

The Problems in Pricing Something New

Pricing a completely new product or service adds many layers of complexity onto an already difficult pricing decision. For example:

- You're competing against known brands (for more on how, see Chapter 15!).

- Buyers don't know your quality.

- Buyers don't have any "feelings" toward your brand.

- Buyers are (most likely) reasonably happy with the brand they've already bought.

- You'll be tempted to undercut your lowest-priced competitor as a reason for buyers to try your brand.

When buyers don't know anything about your brand, they use your price as a strong indication of quality.

Price Equals Quality Buyer Perception

A large number of research studies show that buyers see a relationship between the price of something and its quality.

It is especially true in studies where price is the only difference that can be easily perceived by the consumer.

Attribution theory, originally developed by Heider (1958), states that people infer causation for behaviors. Applying this to a new-product pricing, buyers are likely to attribute causes for a company putting a lower or higher price on its product than is on competitive products.

According to Lichtenstein, Burton, and O'Hara (1989), who tested 34 different attributions as to why a discount was given, consumer attributions fall into three categories, one of which is *attributions due to the product*.

In other words, they may assume the reason you priced your product so low is because you know the quality is poor. Or they may assume the reason you priced your product so high is because you know it is higher quality than competitive products.

In 2005, Dr. Ron Drozdenko (marketing chair at Western Connecticut State University) and I allowed consumers to select the maximum discount level they preferred for their *favorite*

brands in each of eight different product categories. Just 13 percent of consumers took the deepest discount on all products.

We then asked consumers to indicate reasons why they didn't select the largest discount. Here are their reasons, with the frequency of their being cited by consumers:

- Poor quality (54 percent)
- Damaged goods (51 percent)
- Outdated goods (46 percent)
- Old goods (43 percent)
- Knock-offs (33 percent)
- Stolen goods (24 percent)
- Gray market (16 percent)

Does Quality Equal Likelihood-to-Buy?

A higher quality perception doesn't necessarily mean more people are likely to buy it. Petroshius and Monroe (1987) researched products in a product-line offering.

For example, assume buyers see four different inkjet printers from a company:

- $169
- $149
- $129
- $99

This research found that buyers perceive the quality of each of the models to directly correspond to the price (i.e., the $169 printer is the best quality and the $99 is the worst).

But when they asked which was the best value, buyers said it was the $99 model. And when they asked which of the four a buyer would be most likely to buy, they found it to be the lower two price positions.

You need to ask yourself how important quality is to consumers of your product or service—and whether they find current brands lacking. Remember the soap example: While people may agree your soap is 10 percent better quality, almost nobody cares enough to pay a price premium. What they have is good enough, in their perception.

And *their perception* equals *your reality*.

Understanding "Bargain Hunters"

There is a group of consumers in the United States (and probably in other countries) who are full-time bargain hunters. They have no loyalty to a brand and will switch instantly to whoever offers the lowest price. These bargain hunters were identified as early as 1966, when a research study on quality (Gabor and Granger) found a sub-group of bargain shoppers who did not conform to their study's findings. While most consumers in their study were more likely to buy at moderate or low-moderate prices, the researchers found a subset who were not deterred by low prices and who would accept even a ridiculously cheap offer.

These brand switchers seem motivated more by the thrill of the deal than by trying to avoid paying more than necessary. They seem to care more about bragging rights for how little they spent than worrying about the quality of what they buy. Various researchers have pegged this group as comprising anywhere from 15 to 25 percent of shoppers.

This means that if you have the lowest price, you will instantly appeal to those in this group who plan to buy your type of product. But the second another company offers even a few cents less, they will jump to that product.

If you have lower costs than your competitors, this group will love you. And you'll love them.

If you don't have lower costs than your competitors, then it will hurt your profits to try to sell to this group.

Price Preferences by Product Type

Beyond the bargain-hunter personality, other consumers usually restrict bargain shopping to products that aren't important to them. For example Lambert (1972) did an interesting study using only fictitious brands—those that don't exist. The reason for this was to remove any influence from name brands. He offered buyers three choices of products where the only difference was the price, and he tested seven different product categories. Here's what he found:

- Products where consumers selected the cheapest option included toothpaste, coffee, and suntan lotion.
- Products where consumers selected the middle price included tape recorders and molded luggage.
- Products where consumers selected the highest price included portable stereos and tennis racquets.

Lambert concluded that price preferences (in the absence of brand names) were not always for the lowest price and that they were product-specific.

The research also looked at whether buyers experienced in a particular product category were more likely to buy the cheapest choice. Lambert found instead they were more likely to purchase the highest-priced option. This could be biased, as those who rate themselves experienced buyers of, say, tennis racquets are likely to play a lot of tennis and may then prefer a better quality product—which they hope to secure through the higher price.

Detailed Research on Buyer Price Position Preferences

Exhibit 14.1 shows the results of a research study Dr. Ron Drozdenko and I did on the attractiveness of specific price positions for a new product—when brand names were not a factor. We researched 12 different products and offered five different price choices for each.

For example, for a long-sleeve, 100 percent cotton shirt with collar, the price choices were:

- Low ($9)
- Low/middle ($27)
- Middle ($45)
- High/middle ($62)
- High ($79)

Exhibit 14.1 shows the results over all 12 product types. Here is some of the intelligence we can get from this study:

1. The fewest people will purchase the highest-priced alternative.
   a. This is obviously no surprise, but before you discard the idea of making the most expensive brand consider the profit margins for that product. Luxury brands often make more profits on far less sales than do lower-priced brands with far more sales.

2. A large group of people would purchase the lowest price option.

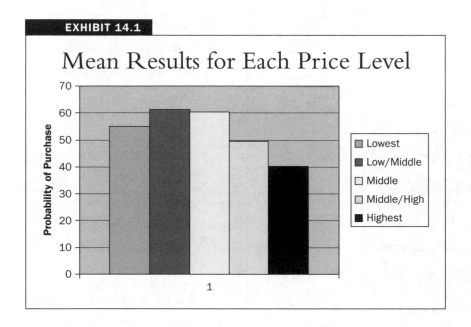

a. Again, no surprise. But consider that a big percentage of these purchasers are bargain shoppers who will never develop a loyalty to your brand. They will switch instantly to anyone with a lower price.

3. Most interesting are the results for low/middle and middle price positions. Here's what stands out:

a. People were more likely to buy either of them than the lowest price option.

■ If so, then why launch with the lower profits you'd get from the cheapest price position?

b. People were equally likely to buy the low/middle and the middle price positions.

■ If so, then why launch at low/middle? Why not instead get the higher profits from the middle position?

Because other research has shown price preferences can differ by the type of product, we then broke out the results by product type. Exhibit 14.2 shows what we found.

What can we learn from Exhibit 14.2? Products for which the cheapest price is most attractive included watches and shirts. In both these categories, not only was the lowest-priced

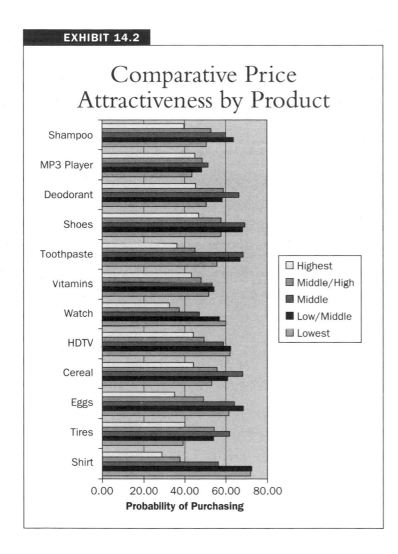

EXHIBIT 14.2

Comparative Price Attractiveness by Product

Shampoo
MP3 Player
Deodorant
Shoes
Toothpaste
Vitamins
Watch
HDTV
Cereal
Eggs
Tires
Shirt

Legend:
☐ Highest
▨ Middle/High
■ Middle
■ Low/Middle
▨ Lowest

0.00   20.00   40.00   60.00   80.00
Probability of Purchasing

option most attractive, but the highest-priced option was least attractive.

Products for which the middle price is most attractive included:

- MP3 player
- Deodorant
- Shoes
- Toothpaste
- Cereal
- Tires

What can we make of consumer preference to pay the middle-of-the-road price for these products instead of a thriftier price?

- First, we must recognize that for deodorant, toothpaste, and cereal the out-of-pocket costs are slight, so upgrading doesn't require as much cash for these products as for some others.

- Deodorant carries a social risk if the product doesn't work, so spending a few more cents for a better-quality deodorant may provide ease of mind.

- The most likely reason for the MP3 player, shoes, toothpaste, and cereal is that consumers have tried

Note

The "lowest-priced option being the most attractive" scenario doesn't mean a high-priced watch or shirt won't succeed. In addition to the success of Rolex, there are a group of watch brands successful at prices four or five times that of Rolex. But they will have to make their profits from a much smaller group of buyers.

cheap brands and found them unsatisfactory. Thus most of these consumers are likely to avoid the cheapest brands in the future.

- Tires carry a physical safety risk. If a tire blows on a freeway, the result could be your life—or at least some physical harm. In that situation, more people seek higher quality, even though the additional cost is substantial.

Additional Research on Preferred Prices

Because this research could be critical for pricing new products, I replicated it for four products in a separate study. Replicating research is one way we test it to make sure the research is valid. The new research verified the results and also offered some new insights.

If you've studied economics in college (or even in high school) you were probably told about a demand curve. This purports to show how demand drops as price rises. It typically looks something like the figure in Exhibit 14.3.

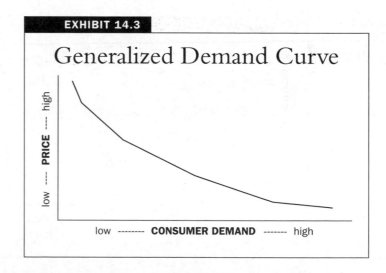

EXHIBIT 14.3

Generalized Demand Curve

Exhibit 14.4 shows the results of the four retested price preferences plotted as demand curves. You'll see the plotted line of the shirt/blouse comes closest to a traditional demand curve, while the other products are very different:

- HDTVs show a small drop at each price increment.

- Vitamins are preferred at the second-from-lowest price level.

- Tires are preferred at the middle level.

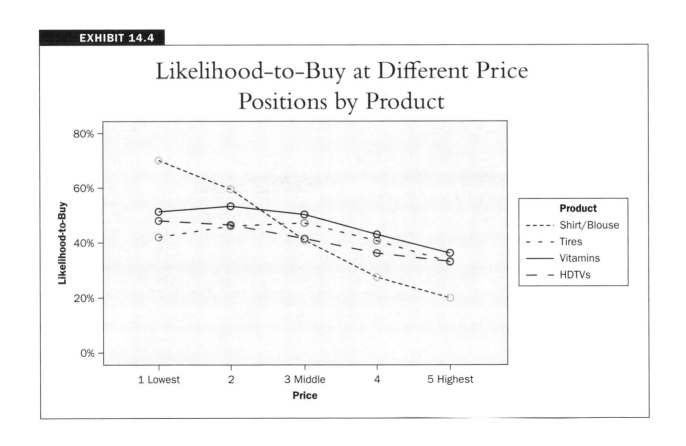

EXHIBIT 14.4

Likelihood-to-Buy at Different Price Positions by Product

Another interesting way to look at this research is to break out the products so we see how diverse the demand is at each level. Note in Exhibit 14.5 that the widest diversity in price preferences is seen for the shirt/blouse. This means a change in price—either up or down—can make a huge difference in demand.

Finally, I looked at the products by the type of risk they carried if a person bought the cheapest one and it didn't work well.

What stood out is consumer sensitivity to a safety/physical risk (see Exhibit 14.6). More consumers preferred the middle or second-highest price levels for the two safety-risk products than they did for the HDTVs.

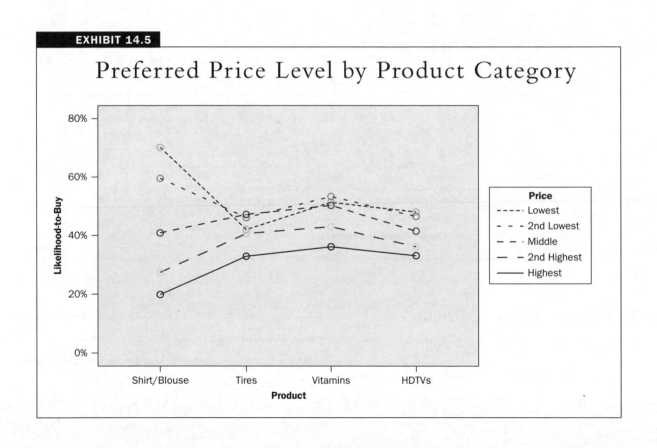

EXHIBIT 14.5

Preferred Price Level by Product Category

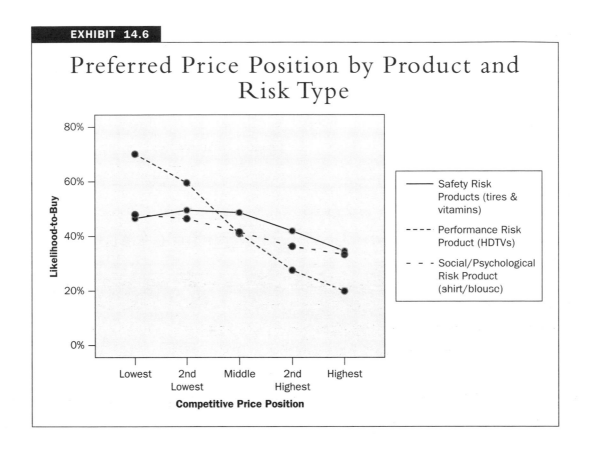

EXHIBIT 14.6

Preferred Price Position by Product and Risk Type

Safety Risk Products (tires & vitamins)

Performance Risk Product (HDTVs)

Social/Psychological Risk Product (shirt/blouse)

Learn More about Risk and Pricing

Dowling (1986) identified aspects of *risk theory*, including:

1. Products can be meaningfully ordered by their risk, and

2. Perceptions change according to a person's wealth position.

In a study of three consumer electronics products (a TV, a stereo, and a camera) Peterson and Wilson (1985) found the higher the price, the less perceived performance risk in consumer perceptions.

Grewal, Gotlieb, and Marmorstein (1994) recommended new brands introduced at lower-than-competitive prices use a highly credible spokesperson to offset an otherwise likely perception of increased performance risk.

This potential use of risk to justify high prices was developed by Bettman (1973). He recommended marketers with high-priced products emphasize the risks of their product category while also stressing the quality of their own brands.

Looking at risk—without looking at it specifically by product—may underestimate its effect in consumer reactions to price. This is consistent with the theory of risk taking in consumer behavior proposed by Taylor (1974). Taylor noted that research must be purchase specific, and that it may be difficult or impossible to generalize across studies with different products.

Tellis (1988) also found a correlation between risk perception and optimal prices or discounts.

Of course, most new products or services have direct competitors—usually with established brand names. The next chapter looks at competing against established brands.

CHAPTER 15

Pricing New Products/Services, Part 2

Competing with Established Brands

In-a-Rush Tip

You can skip this chapter if you are re-pricing established products or services.

You can also skip it if you need a price today.

But . . . if you are pricing a new product in a marketplace with established brands, this chapter will help you price more profitably.

When Your Competitors Are Established Brands

Unfortunately, new brands usually enter markets where they must compete with established brands. That conveys a whole list (following) of advantages for the established brands and only a couple of advantages for the unknown brands.

Established brands are said to have "equity" in their brand name. One of the better definitions of brand equity is that it represents the difference in consumer response to marketing activity for one brand over another, or over an unknown brand (Keller, 1993; Hoeffler and Keller, 2003).

That difference can be either positive or negative, with the latter leading to negative brand equity.

Following are itemized the many advantages known brands command. It is critical to know what these are before deciding on the price for your new brand, because they affect how consumers will react to your brand and price.

Advantages for Known Brands

Known (and respected) brands command a large number of advantages over unknown brands. They include the following:

Increased Learning of New Content

When buyers recognize a brand, they are more likely to learn about new products from that brand. Johnson and Russo (1984) found increased learning of new features and new ad copy for the familiar brand.

This means as a new brand your ads touting your better features (or price) will have to be more noticeable than those for established brands.

More Likely to Consider the Brand

We're all lazy. When we decide to buy a new product, very few of us consider all possible brands. Simonson, Huber, and Payne (1988) found that consumers will first focus on the most attractive (known) brands and only later consider lesser or unknown brands.

Be wary of research that appears to contradict these findings. The researchers found this process exists only in making a choice, not when asked to rank brands. If research asks consumers to rank brands in a field, consumers first consider moderately attractive or second-tier brands. Thus ranking research will overestimate the attention given to mid-level brands.

The only ways to somewhat alleviate this problem are to create more noticeable promotions and to be extremely clear and on message as to your benefits over established products/services.

Reduced Search Time

Because we're all lazy, that means we want to spend less time researching the quality of our choices. For those seeking quality merchandise, Dodds, Monroe, and Grewal (1991) found that a brand name, a high price, and availability in a quality retail store all communicate quality to consumers. These days another quality verifier is the customer reviews on web sites. All these quality cues can reduce the amount of search consumers feel is necessary before buying.

As a new brand, this means if you can match two or three of the four, consumers will be reassured of your quality—even without the recognized brand name.

Increased Attention

Tellis (1988) found that consumers pay more attention to messages from preferred brands, which leads to increased responsiveness to those brands. Again, it shows messages from new brands need to stand out better just to get noticed.

Focal Brands

When we compare a group of brands, we typical start with a "focal" brand—a brand to which we compare the others. An established brand, with higher awareness and feature recall, is more likely to be the focal brand. And a focal brand is more attractive than the others, unless the others give powerful reasons to switch focus. Dhar and Simonson (1992) did some interesting research in this area.

There's nothing really a new brand can do here. It's a problem for second-tier established brands as well; it's one of the benefits of being the leading brand in a category.

Positive Attitude Carryover

Established brands carry a positive attitude that affects consumer response to them. A number of research studies have backed up this finding, including the following.

Affects Reaction to Ads   Raj and Stoner (1996) showed consumers mocked-up ads for State Farm and an unknown competitor, as well as for Kinko's and an unknown competitor. When asked their likelihood to switch from a current provider to either of the others, the scores were significantly higher for the known brands:

Insurance		Copier Services	
State Farm	3.42	Kinko's	4.79
Unknown brand	1.98	Unknown brand	3.09

Affects Both Quality Ratings and Purchase Intentions   A number of research studies show that a brand name can be seen as a "guarantor" of quality. In fact, in most cases, consumers will choose a brand name as being a better indicator of quality than is a higher price (Monroe, 1973).

I and Dr. Drozdenko (2004) studied known brands versus unknown brands in five product categories. We found the known brand in each category had both higher quality and higher likelihood-to-buy ratings.

Dawar and Parker (1994) found brand name signals to be the most important factor for consumers in determining product quality. Price and physical appearance were the next most important, followed by retailer reputation.

So what does this mean for new products/services where quality is an important selection criterion for buyers? It means you:

- Are at a disadvantage (no surprise here!)
- Need to use the remaining tools at your disposal very carefully to project the quality image you're seeking

  - Your price needs to say "quality."
  - Your physical appearance of the product (or the service environment) is even more important than for established brands.
  - Your actual quality will be critical, if consumers post reviews of products in your category.

Affects How Buyers React to Humor(!)   As a crazy example of just how powerful brand reactions can be, Chattopadhyay and Basu (1990) found that humorous ads are less effective for unknown brands!

They found that new product/service ads require greater attention and learning from buyers, and the humor in those ads draws attention away from the product. That's not a problem if buyers already know about the brand, but it is a big problem when it causes buyers to skip paying needed attention to learning about a new product/ service.

What can you do? Save the humor in your promotions until buyers are aware of your product/service brand.

Risk Avoidance

If you're launching a new product/service, there are some very disturbing research results in the area of risk avoidance—especially for "performance risk." Performance risk is the risk that what we buy won't work (or won't work well) and we might be stuck with a poor product.

We're not surprised that consumer perceptions of the performance risk of a product from an unknown brand are greater than for a known brand (Grewal, Gotlieb, and Marmorstein, 1994). That makes sense.

However, Muthukrishnam (1995) pushed this further by studying an unknown brand compared to a known brand that was markedly inferior. Here are the disheartening results:

- When no product trial was available, 65 percent of the subjects chose the known, inferior brand over the unknown brand.
- When a free trial was offered, 39 percent *still* chose the known and inferior brand.
- Half of those who chose the known brand were extremely confident that it was superior—despite very clear indications it was inferior.

- Even worse—38 percent of those who chose the known brand *agreed* that the unknown brand was superior, demonstrating a strong risk aversion by going with the known even in the face of superior attributes.

What can entrepreneurs do in the face of such disheartening results? Here are some suggestions:

- Offer some sort of free trial if at all possible (it almost doubled the number who would try the new brand).

- Offer the strongest guarantee you can as to performance. Let buyers know how easy it would be to return the product/cancel the service if they weren't 100 percent satisfied.

- Offer extensive details on your quality and on the specifics of what you offer.

- If you can, get other people to verify how much better your product/service is than the competition, as in testimonials. Just note that believable testimonials contain the full name of the recommender.

  - When businesspeople are doing the recommending, a link to their web sites is a gold standard of believability. And it increases the chance of getting the testimonial, as it would be an incoming link that could help their site's Google ranking.

  - Individuals as testimonial providers are less believable, so be sure to add specifics in the testimonial to increase believability.

Price Premiums for Known Brands

Top-tier brands can usually command a price premium over their competitors. The size of the brand advantage for Hewlett Packard laser printers was researched by Crowley and Zajas (1996). They noted that Hewlett Packard typically maintained a 10–20 percent price premium over competitors, despite a market share of over 60 percent. They also noted that in 1990–1991, low-priced competitors cut their prices, which caused the price premium for Hewlett Packard to climb over 20 percent, at which point Hewlett Packard lost 13 points of market share.

So while consumers are willing to pay more for quality brands, there's a limit to the size of that premium—at least for some buyers.

Brand-loyal customers have a wider range of acceptable prices (Kalyanaram and Little, 1994). These researchers argue that brand-loyal customers believe whatever their preferred brand charges is "normal." They then judge other brand prices by their difference (up or down) from whatever their preferred brand's price is.

Following is some research I did with Dr. Ron Dro-zdenko to try to uncover just how substantial a benefit a name brand has over an unknown brand—particularly at different price levels for the unknown brand.

We found the difference in buyers willing to buy a new brand dropped 17 percent (across four product categories) when an established brand was available. See Exhibit 15.1. When we looked at it by product category, entering a market with a name brand competitor caused anywhere from a 10–20 percent decline in intent-to-buy.

We were also interested in any differences depending on what price positioning the new brand had. Did it compete

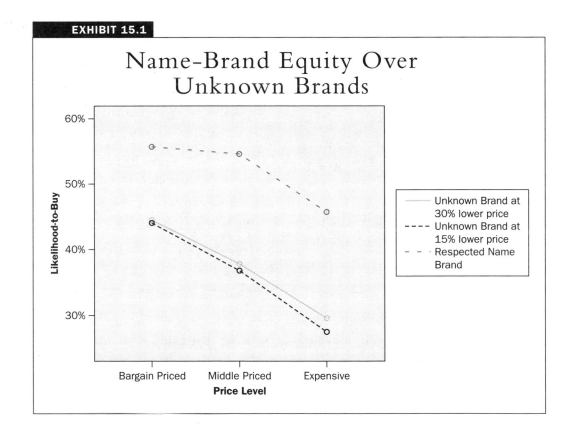

EXHIBIT 15.1

Name-Brand Equity Over Unknown Brands

against bargain name brands? Middle-of-the-road name brands? Premium name brands?

We found for a shirt/blouse and for HDTVs, an unknown brand came closer in selection to a name in the bargain-price than in higher-price categories. For vitamins, it was the opposite: It was easier for the unknown brand to compete in the premium categories.

Exhibits 15.2, 15.3, and 15.4 show the details of what we found.

In a wild leap of hopeful thinking on my part, we also looked at how a higher-priced unknown brand would do against a 15 percent lower priced brand name. (I'd found just one research study to suggest there might be positive news in this scenario.)

Unfortunately, hope wasn't supported by the facts, although shirts/blouses and vitamins had a smaller difference between the two than the other two product categories. See Exhibit 15.5.

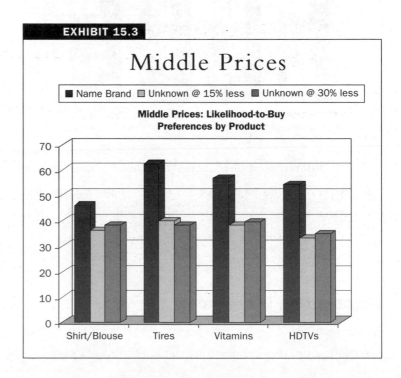

EXHIBIT 15.2

Bargain Prices

Bargain Prices: Likelihood-to-Buy Preferences by Product

■ Name Brand ☐ Unknown @ 15% less ■ Unknown @ 30% less

EXHIBIT 15.3

Middle Prices

Middle Prices: Likelihood-to-Buy Preferences by Product

■ Name Brand ☐ Unknown @ 15% less ■ Unknown @ 30% less

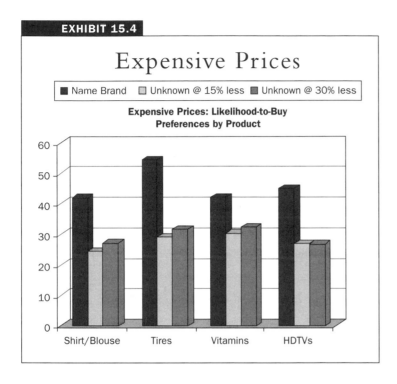

EXHIBIT 15.4

Expensive Prices

■ Name Brand ☐ Unknown @ 15% less ■ Unknown @ 30% less

**Expensive Prices: Likelihood-to-Buy
Preferences by Product**

The difference applied across all three price position categories, although a 15 percent higher-priced product competing against bargain-positioned name brands had a better chance of success than it did in the higher price positions. (See Exhibit 15.6.)

Discounting Differences

A large number of research studies show that price promotions (discounts) from top-tier brands attract purchasers of lower-level brands. Those studies also show the reverse is not true: Lower-level brand promotions do not equally attract purchasers of top-tier brands (Agrawal, 1996; Sivakumar and Raj, 1997; Park and Srinivasan, 1994; Blattberg and Wisniewski, 1989).

Unknown brands need to be wary of discounts. For example, Moore and Olshavsky (1989) found a positive buyer response to all levels of discounts for name brands, but found a negative response at the highest level (75 percent) for unknown brands.

Advantages for *Unknown* Brands (Yes, There Are a Few!)

There are a few positives for unknown brands, although many of them are just groups that are more likely to be adventurous and try a new brand.

Look for "Innovators"

Just as there is a group of "bargain hunters" who love the thrill of finding a deal, there is also a group of "innovators" who are thrilled by finding something new.

The only problem is there are fewer innovators (estimated at 2–3 percent of the population) than bargain shoppers. Nevertheless, this group does exist and you can profit if you can identify and promote to them when you launch a new product/service.

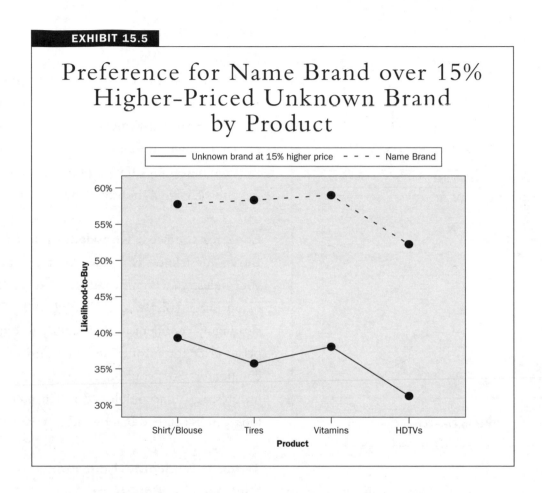

EXHIBIT 15.5

Preference for Name Brand over 15% Higher-Priced Unknown Brand by Product

——— Unknown brand at 15% higher price   - - - - Name Brand

Likelihood-to-Buy

Product: Shirt/Blouse, Tires, Vitamins, HDTVs

Of course, that assumes your product/service is actually new, not just the same old thing everyone else is selling—but a new brand name. This group will not be impressed by something "new" that really isn't.

Finding innovators is typically a problem. In some markets it's almost impossible. In others, the innovators are professionals who will expect payment for using your products and letting others know it. (Think snowboards, tennis racquets, etc.)

EXHIBIT 15.6

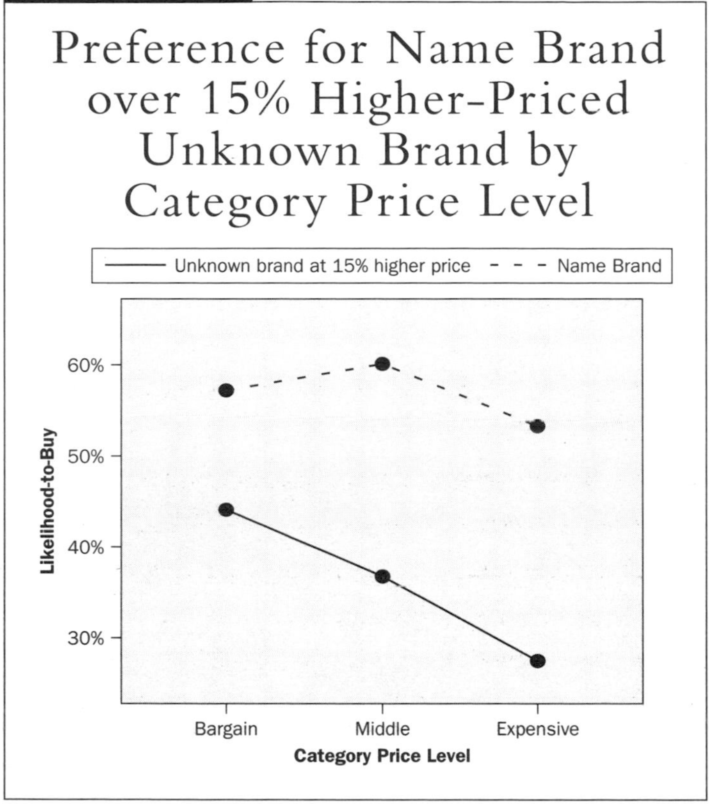
Preference for Name Brand over 15% Higher-Priced Unknown Brand by Category Price Level
Unknown brand at 15% higher price
Name Brand
60%
50%
40%
30%
Likelihood-to-Buy
Bargain
Middle
Expensive
Category Price Level

One way to search for them is to rent mailing lists of people who bought the last new thing—at the start. For example, let's say your new product is product "C," which came after and improved upon products "A" and "B" in your industry. Try to find a direct mail list of people who bought "B" when it first launched.

People (latest estimates are at 500,000 or so) who promote for buzz marketing type firms are also people who want to know what's new. These firms typically don't pay money to their promoters. Instead they get free samples of the latest new things. If your product is national and you have the budget, you might profit from accessing their promoters.

Look for the Most Knowledgeable Buyers

Buyers most knowledgeable about products or services in your industry are significantly less likely to be influenced by brand image (Biswas and Sherrell, 1993). These buyers are also highly confident in their ability to estimate the appropriate price for an offering based on its features relative to competitors. So if your product is priced appropriately for its features, as you accomplished in Chapter 6, this group will look past established brands and give you a fair opportunity.

Target Low Income/Education *or* High Income/Education

New brands may have more chance when aimed at low-income and/or education segments, or at high-income and education segments.

Chance and French (1972) surveyed consumers about their willingness to switch grocery brands for a lower price. They first asked subjects for brand preferences in seven different product types. Then they asked how big a price break they would want to switch to a different brand. The most interesting result from this study was a U-shaped response over both income categories and education.

The lowest and the highest income and education groups were more willing to switch for a much smaller price break than those in the middle income or education groups. Further, the education effect persisted independent of income levels.

The raises the question of whether middle income and middle education groups are more conservative and more brand-dependent.

Target Infrequent Buyers

While we all want to sell to heavy purchasers in our categories, some research suggests that infrequent buyers might be a better target when your brand is new. For example, Gonul, Leszczyc, and Sugawara (1996) found that the less frequently a household purchases ketchup, the more likely it will switch brands.

Coupons Work—with Some Dangers!

The method you use to cause brand switching can affect both the number of switchers and subsequent sales.

Media-distributed coupons generated the most brand switching, compared to cents-off deals and package coupons (Dodson, Tybout, and Sternthal, 1978).

However, when these coupons are withdrawn, not only do the switchers leave, *but significantly more of the brand-loyal buyers also leave!* Of course, as a new brand you don't have brand-loyal buyers, so this is more a danger to worry about once you are more established.

The authors recommend cents-off marked deals instead. Cents-off deals do cause brand switching (although less than media-distributed coupons) without the dramatic falloff in repeat sales.

Really High Prices Are More Believable (!)

There's a lot of research on what is termed "implausible external reference prices" that is intriguing when it comes to known versus unknown brands.

When faced with startling high (implausible) prices, consumers tend to discount them. This is especially apparent when you see a "Was $1,000/Now $500" type of promotion. The $1,000 is discounted as not believable.

But consumers are less likely to discount such a price for an unfamiliar brand than they are for a known brand (Biswas and Blair, 1991). The researchers conclude that consumers heavily discount an implausible price for a familiar brand, to bring it closer to their (more strongly held) prior estimates. Thus, implausibly high advertised prices are more believable when paired with an unknown brand.

Even more interesting, they found that an implausibly high price resulted in higher shopping intention (intent-to-buy) for unfamiliar than for familiar brands.

This indicates a potential high-end price positioning niche for unknown brands. I've done some preliminary research in this area and found unknown brands priced higher than established brands do *not* attract more buyers than the known brand. But there is some preliminary evidence that the penalty you pay for being unknown is less in the highest price positions than in middle to lower ones.

What Causes Customers to Switch to a New Brand?

A new brand almost always requires a buyer to switch from an established brand in order to make a sale. For that reason, we can learn from research on brand switching—even though much of the research is about switching from one known brand to another.

The only time new brands don't require switching is when your new brand creates a "blue ocean" where there are no competitors. For example, [yellow tail] wines created a strategy that caused it to appeal to people who were not previously wine drinkers. For a great read and lots of ideas, I definitely recommend you read Kim and Mauborgne's book *Blue Ocean Strategy.*

Factors for Switching

A lower price isn't the only reason for switching to a new brand. Dr. Drozdenko and I in 2003 examined many reasons for switching from a preferred brand to a new brand. Exhibit 15.7 shows what we found when we looked at toothpaste.

EXHIBIT 15.7 CAUSES OF BRAND SWITCHING	
Factors Causing a Switch to an Unknown Toothpaste Brand	**Mean**
Try it free offer	7.545
Am. Dental Assn. recommends it	5.969
Save 30% over your regular brand	5.735
Ranked #1 by *Consumer Reports*	4.980
Latest scientific advance	4.876
Research study says it's the best	4.848
All new!	4.743
Your brand had a recall (now corrected)	4.339
Save 15% over your regular brand	4.234
Better for the environment than your brand	3.896
Endorsement by a celebrity	3.697

We found differences in younger consumers compared to older. Younger buyers were more likely overall to be willing to switch. And they were especially likely to switch if:

- A new offer is available.

- Their preferred brand was once recalled.

- A new brand has extra features.

- Their preferred brand comes out with an ad they hate.

We also found females were more likely to switch than males after seeing an ad for another product.

Likelihood to Switch

When a customer enters a store intending to buy one brand, what is the likelihood of that person switching brands? There is a fair amount of research on grocery shopping and brand switching. For example, Cavallo and Temares (1969) found 18–21 percent of grocery shoppers switched brands inside the store. They further broke it out as follows:

- Buyers of canned and frozen vegetables switched 21 percent of the time.

- Buyers of soaps/detergents switched 19 percent of the time.

- Those buying beverages switched 18 percent of the time.

Convenience

Convenience also plays a role in causing brand switching. Cavallo and Temares also found that 19 percent of shoppers who enter a store expecting to buy a preferred brand actually walk out with a different brand.

They also asked shoppers what they would do if their preferred brand was not in the store. Given this scenario, 59 percent of all subjects said they would purchase another brand.

Of that 59 percent, however, 23 percent of these buyers had rated the strength of their brand preference as moderate to poor ("4" to "7" on a seven-point scale where "1" is the strongest preference).

Of those who gave their brand preference the highest rating, just 31 percent said they would buy another brand if theirs was not in the store.

Still, that means 31 percent of the most loyal buyers of a brand *are* willing to switch for convenience.

Doing What Others Do

Ever wonder why the heck advertisements state their popularity? "We're #1—more buyers choose us than any other brand."

If your answer (like mine) to that is "So what? Who cares?" you'll be surprised to know that research shows *a lot* of people care.

Wanting to fit in with others can cause buyers to switch to more "popular" brands. For example, Weber and Hansen (1972) found 46 percent of housewives would switch from their *preferred* brands to brands they were told were the preferred brands of other housewives in the study.

This willingness to switch was the same over six different product categories, including food items and toothpaste.

Regret and Switching

When people chose products/services under uncertainty (such as when it's an unfamiliar brand), regret theory says they will try to anticipate possible regret and act to avoid it (Loomes and Sugden, 1982).

One problem for entrepreneurs is that switching produces more regret than staying with a current brand, because the status quo is more "normal" (Kahneman and Miller, 1986).

The reasons for a buyer switching brands affected regret and in some cases reversed the normal finding of more regret for switching than for not. If prior experiences with the current brand were bad, consumers felt less regret if they switched than if they didn't. And this was true even if the new brand also proved unsatisfactory (Inman and Zeelenberg, 2002).

What Happens *after* Buyers Switch?

Assuming you can get customers to try your new brand, how likely are you to hold onto them? Lawrence (1969) looked at grocery scanner data for toothpaste purchases over time. Here are some of his findings:

- Consumers who bought the same brand at least five times in one year and then switched
  - 31 percent reverted back to the first brand after a single switch.
  - 43 percent reverted back if they had bought the first brand 10 or more times.
- 22 percent of the switchers became vacillators, equally likely to buy the original brand or the second brand.
- 12–14 percent became loyal buyers of the new brand.

Lawrence also found that switching once seems to set up a brand-switching frenzy in some consumers, who then go on to try yet a third brand. They are:

- 35 percent of those who previously had medium loyalty to the first brand
- 21 percent of those who had previously bought the first brand more than 10 times consecutively

Did the switching reason affect whether or not the buyer developed a loyalty to the new brand? A price promotion was involved in:

- 10–20 percent of those who became no longer loyal to the first brand
- 37 percent of the switchers who then reverted back to the first brand

Shocking Findings on Brand Names

If you ever have the time for a trip into LaLa Land, you might want to research "false fame" when it comes to brand names.

Apparently, it is very important that consumers believe they recognize your brand name, even if they don't. Holden and Vanhuele (1999) found that merely hearing fictitious brand names in a product category—for example, being told these names were being *considered* for a new product—resulted a day (or seven days) later to subjects being more than twice as likely to list those brands as established compared to fictitious names that were not previously mentioned.

This is important because familiar brands tend to be favored in choice situations. One of the key aspects of this research is that consumers will remember the brand names, but not the situation within which they heard the brand name; else they would remember that those brands were nonexistent.

The same results have been found when researchers have someone memorize a list of names as a memory test. A week after the memory test, subjects are more likely to "recognize" names on that list and believe them to be established brands.

Baker (1999) found that mere exposure to brand names can have strong effects on which brand will be chosen. Thus a promoted name will cause a new or low-share product to be preferred over other new or low-share equivalent-attribute brands.

So What Does it All Mean for Pricing a New Product/Service?

After reading this chapter, doesn't it seem almost miraculous that new brands can enter the market and succeed? Yet they can and do. And you can, too.

I believe the major factor in success comes down to positioning. Here are some key questions to ask to best determine your positioning, and therefore your price:

1. Is there a hole in the market? Is one of the positioning strategies vacant? Is there a premium price/quality option? Is there a cheap, low-feature option? If either of those positions is vacant *and* your company is capable of creating products/services in the vacant position, then filling that "hole" will increase your odds of success.

2. Is there some reason why your costs are much lower than the competitors? Some *sustainable* reason? If so, enter at the penetration (cheap) position. You'll be able to grab all the bargain hunter buyers who seek the cheapest price and you'll get your foot in the market.

You don't have to stay in the cheap position forever. For example, Japanese automakers entered the U.S. market in the cheap position. From there they became recognized for quality products, and were able to add more and more expensive cars. Today they reap luxury profits for Acura and Lexus.

3. Is there some reasonable-sized group of buyers in your product field that would like different features? Example: If everyone is selling the same types of swim goggles, you could specialize in swim goggles for tri-athletes, with added features appropriate for their sport. Yes, you'd have a smaller target group of buyers, but you'd be their *first* choice—not just an also-ran in the bigger marketplace.

4. If there's no hole in the market positioning, your costs are not sustainably lower, and there's no subset of buyers for you to focus on, then your entry—and chances for success—will be more difficult.

Based on all this research, it appears your best positioning strategy is competitive, anywhere from low to high competitive. You'll need the extra profits per unit to differentiate your product/service in some manner that matters to the buyer. This could be through additional features, easier payment options, or a psychological positioning (e.g., your product is more appealing to young trendsetters) that will require extensive promotional efforts.

CHAPTER 16

Pricing with Discounts

In-a-Rush Tip

You can skip this chapter if you are not currently dealing with discounts.

You also can skip it if you need to set a price today. But . . . discounts can have a big effect on the best price—a big positive *or* negative effect.

Discounts: A Double-Edged Sword

Psychologically, we all love discounts—poor and wealthy alike. We like to think we're getting a deal. That we're lucky. Or that we're a smart shopper.

Discounts *almost* always increase unit sales. The "almost" reflects big questions about when you have a premium-quality product or when consumers have little method other than price by which to judge your quality—*and* quality is extremely important to them.

So should you offer them? It depends. Remember when I said what people hate about marketers is our answer to everything is to test it? Well, that's the correct answer here.

If you don't test the effect of discounts, you may be throwing away a lot of money. You'll see in some of the research that follows that:

- Discounts can worry consumers enough that they'll reject your product/service.

- You may get no more sales from a 40 percent discount than a 30 percent discount. Or you may get no more sales from a 30 percent discount than a 20 percent discount. (Or you might!)

- The discounts your consumers will respond to most will be different depending on:

  - Your industry

  - Your competitors

  - Whether you are a known brand or not

  - The age of your target customers

  - The income levels of your target customers

When Discounts Worry Consumers

We all want the biggest discounts we can get. Correct? Not really!

Dr. Ron Drozdenko and I did a research study where we asked consumers to tell us the *maximum* discount they would *accept*(!) for eight different products. Their choices were 10 percent up to 80 percent.

We were stunned to find just 13 percent of respondents accepted the highest discount (80 percent) for every product category. Further, in none of the eight different product categories did more than 42 percent of respondents select the highest discount.

This is especially eye-opening since these were not discounts from some hypothetical list price; our research showed buyers the exact dollar price reductions they would get at each level for each product.

Exhibit 16.1 shows the average results by product. Notice how surprisingly close to 50 percent the average preferred discount is. Tires had the lowest acceptable maximum discount (40 percent average). Buyers were probably worried about poor quality tires, since their personal safety is at risk.

An HDTV (48.5 percent average) and cereal (48.6 percent average) were the products with the next lowest acceptable maximum discounts. With so much to save in a high priced (list $3,833 in the study) product, we expected buyers to go for much bigger discounts. But if the HDTV were to be poor quality, it would be a very poor, upsetting purchase they'd be stuck with for a long time.

When considering the buyer caution with cereal, we theorized a discount of greater than 49 percent might signal a potential risk of spoiled, old, or non-palatable food.

The shirt (59 percent average) had the highest acceptable maximum discount. Buyers are accustomed to the easy return of unsatisfactory clothing, so they may have perceived little risk if the quality was unsatisfactory.

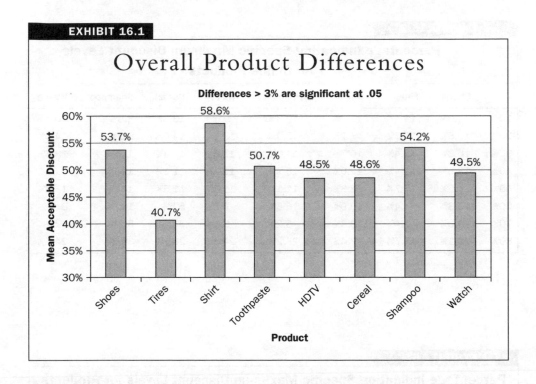

EXHIBIT 16.1

Overall Product Differences

Differences > 3% are significant at .05

Mean Acceptable Discount

- Shoes: 53.7%
- Tires: 40.7%
- Shirt: 58.6%
- Toothpaste: 50.7%
- HDTV: 48.5%
- Cereal: 48.6%
- Shampoo: 54.2%
- Watch: 49.5%

Product

Shampoo (54 percent average) received the second highest maximum acceptable discount. It appears buyers see a relatively low risk in purchasing and using shampoo. The price is relatively low, and if they don't like it they can trash it and purchase something else. See Exhibit 16.1.

Exhibits 16.2 and 16.3 show the percentage of people preferring each different level for each product. The first is for an online sale and the second is for a local retailer.

For online shopping, it's interesting to note the following:

- A 10-percent discount doesn't excite much—except for tires.

- A surprisingly uniform number of people prefer 20 percent, 30 percent, 40 percent, and 50 percent as a discount.

- After 50 percent, you're reaching bargain shoppers who want the maximum.

EXHIBIT 16.2

Percentage Indicating Specific Maximum Discount Levels for Online Products

	Shoes	Tires	Shirt	Toothpaste	HDTV	Cereal	Shampoo	Watch
10%	2.6%	19.4%	1.7%	10.3%	9.6%	13.8%	8.5%	10.1%
20%	10.5%	17.7%	7.2%	13.3%	15.5%	14.0%	6.3%	14.4%
30%	16.8%	16.4%	10.7%	14.6%	13.6%	12.4%	12.9%	13.8%
40%	13.5%	11.4%	12.0%	10.7%	12.5%	11.6%	12.2%	9.6%
50%	14.2%	10.7%	13.8%	11.1%	11.8%	11.6%	14.0%	13.8%
60%	10.3%	4.4%	10.9%	6.6%	7.7%	5.5%	10.3%	8.1%
70%	5.0%	2.4%	10.3%	5.2%	5.0%	3.1%	5.5%	5.5%
80%	27.1%	17.7%	33.4%	28.2%	24.3%	28.2%	30.3%	24.7%

EXHIBIT 16.3

Percentage Indicating Specific Maximum Discount Levels for Products from a Local Retailer

	Shoes	Tires	Shirt	Toothpaste	HDTV	Cereal	Shampoo	Watch
10%	0.7%	10.0%	1.3%	6.5%	3.1%	8.3%	4.8%	3.1%
20%	5.7%	17.7%	3.3%	8.7%	10.7%	11.1%	6.3%	9.6%
30%	12.4%	17.5%	8.9%	13.1%	15.5%	12.0%	11.5%	16.2%
40%	11.8%	12.7%	10.2%	11.1%	14.2%	10.5%	11.1%	12.9%
50%	18.1%	10.5%	11.5%	11.1%	14.2%	11.1%	11.1%	15.1%
60%	12.0%	7.2%	11.5%	9.8%	10.9%	10.2%	9.8%	8.3%
70%	7.6%	3.3%	11.8%	7.2%	5.5%	6.1%	8.3%	7.0%
80%	31.8%	21.2%	41.4%	32.5%	26.0%	30.7%	37.0%	27.9%

If the products were being sold in a local store, people wanted a slightly higher discount level. This tells us the local store is offsetting some of the risk customers see with higher discounts and with online shopping.

Comparing these two situations, it's obvious that online retailers carry more risk in people's minds as to the quality of products being sold.

We also wondered if there were gender, age, or income differences. We found some differences between males and females, but not enough to be statistically significant. Age, however, was significant. Younger consumers reacted more positively to higher discounts, as did those with lower incomes. See Exhibits 16.4 and 16.5.

What Worries Consumers about Discounts

So why would only 13 percent of consumers accept the highest discounts? We asked them that question. Exhibit 16.6 shows the answers they gave. You can see from several of the reasons

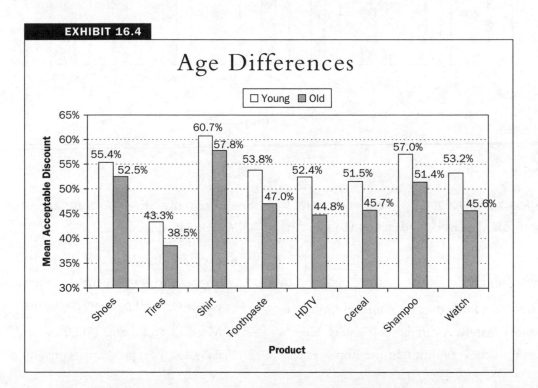

EXHIBIT 16.4

Age Differences

☐ Young ■ Old

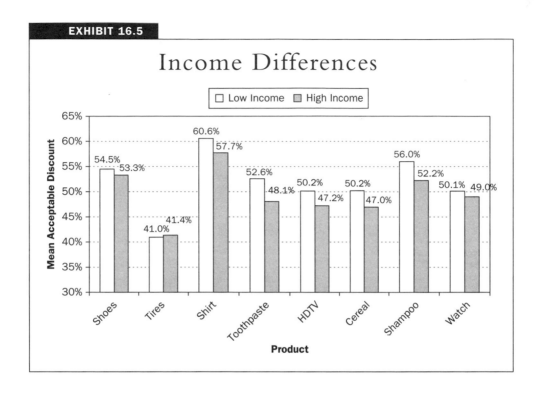

EXHIBIT 16.5

Income Differences

☐ Low Income　■ High Income

Mean Acceptable Discount

- Shoes: 54.5% / 53.3%
- Tires: 41.0% / 41.4%
- Shirt: 60.6% / 57.7%
- Toothpaste: 52.6% / 48.1%
- HDTV: 50.2% / 47.2%
- Cereal: 50.2% / 47.0%
- Shampoo: 56.0% / 52.2%
- Watch: 50.1% / 49.0%

Product

that consumers expect a product at an 80 percent discount to be inferior (knockoffs, old, damaged, outdated, and bad quality):

What Other Studies Say

A number of studies have looked at consumer responses to discounts, with, unfortunately, contradictory results. Here is a summary of several of their findings, in the hopes at least

one or two may give you some ideas more specific to your industry and situation.

- Mobley, Bearden, and Teel (1988) found a positive response to 25 percent discounts, and a more positive response to 50 percent discounts.

- Marshall and Leng (2002) found the same for *product* sales. For products, consumers showed a greater

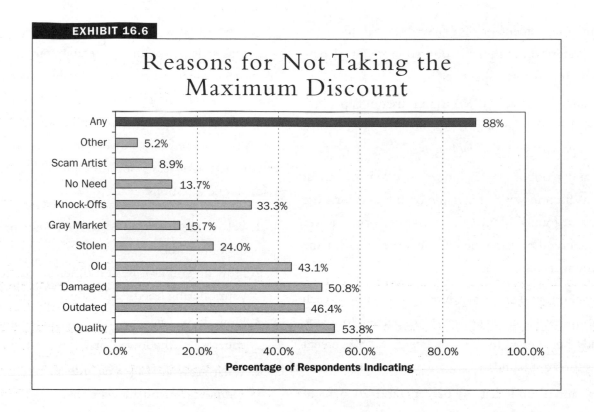

EXHIBIT 16.6

Reasons for Not Taking the Maximum Discount

Reason	Percentage
Any	88%
Other	5.2%
Scam Artist	8.9%
No Need	13.7%
Knock-Offs	33.3%
Gray Market	15.7%
Stolen	24.0%
Old	43.1%
Damaged	50.8%
Outdated	46.4%
Quality	53.8%

Percentage of Respondents Indicating

intent to buy at each discount step (from 10 percent to 50 percent in 10–point increments). At higher levels (moving to a 60 percent or 70 percent discount), they found no significant increase in intent to buy.

- For the sales of *services,* however, Marshall and Leng found that 40–70 percent discounts were perceived

no more positively than 20 percent discounts, while 30 percent garnered the most intent to buy.

- Madan and Suri (2001) found 61 percent of consumers preferred a price presented as a 30 percent discount from list—over the same price without any perceived discount. However, when the authors presented a

discount of 2 percent or 45 percent, they found consumers preferred the non-discounted price (at 61 percent and 75 percent, respectively).

- Moore and Olshavsky (1989) found discounts positive
  at all levels for name brands, but *negative at the highest
  levels (75 percent) for unknown brands.*

- Gupta and Cooper (1992) looked at intent to buy at
  different discount levels for name brands and for store
  brands, and found intent to buy was uniformly lower
  for store brands, even when those stores were name
  department stores.

  - They also found consumer intent to buy rose at each
    discount level from 10 percent to 70 percent for name
    brands, but dipped in the 40 percent and 50 percent
    levels for store brands.

  - They also found that 10 percent and 20 percent
    discount levels for store brands had little positive
    effect.

Determining Best Discount Levels

Discounts signal to buyers at least two things: They can save
money *but* there may be some problem with the product/
service (especially if the discount is larger).

Buyers often will accept an older model, factory second,
last year's style, an unknown retailer, etc. for a lower price.
However, while this tradeoff may be acceptable for some
products like clothing, is it acceptable for other products that
may have safety or other types of risks?

Almost all research shows consumers are more likely to
buy if there is at least some discount. This leaves marketers
with several questions:

1. What's the best (most profitable, not most purchased)
   discount level?
2. How do you *decrease* consumer perceptions of risk—if
   your offering has the lowest price or highest discounts?
3. How do you *increase* consumer perception of risks—if
   yours is not the lowest price/highest discount?
4. What are your *long-term risks* in offering discounts—
   and how can you alleviate them?

The best way to determine your optimal discount levels
is to systematically test alternatives. This is a normal, inex-
pensive, and ongoing process for direct marketers, who rou-
tinely test pricing and discount levels.

For on-ground establishments, marketers may use
matched geographic test markets or simulated test markets
to set prices. Or they may hire outside pricing consultants.

Department stores (usually for fashion) and a few "off-price" retailers use progressive discounts dependent on the time the product is on the shelf. Discounts increase as the time on the shelf increases. Thus a product that hasn't sold in 15 days may see a 5 percent discount; 30 days a 10 percent discount; 45 days a 20 percent discount; etc. This discount method can minimize losses by using the market response to specific products to determine their real value to consumers.

However, with time pressures to increase sales, marketers often use less-systematic methods to determine discounts. Discounts may be set based on industry convention, competitive response, or historical precedence. Using these unscientific methods of setting discounts may cause least two problems:

1. Even if a specific discount they select "works" (it sells X units or increases sales by X percent), the marketer doesn't know if a smaller discount would have achieved similar sales but with higher profits.

2. Deeper discounts may be associated with a lower perception of quality. This lowered quality perception may affect brand loyalty. Many national marketers who used coupons aggressively in past decades moved to "everyday low pricing" policies because they believed discount coupons eroded brand loyalty.

Discounts' Effect on Quality Ratings and Purchase

Because of concerns about how different discount levels affect not just quality perceptions—but actual purchase decisions—Dr. Ron Drozdenko and I conducted a different study. We looked at 15 percent, 30 percent, and 45 percent discount levels.

The top line of the graph in Exhibit 16.7 shows consumer perceptions of the quality of the product, based solely on the discount level. As you can see, there is no significant difference until you have a 45 percent discount, at which time the quality perception dropped.

The average intent to purchase the product went up when there was a 15 percent or 30 percent discount (although no difference in intent between those two), then dropped significantly at a 45 percent discount level.

While the research is contradictory on this, I'd recommend anyone offering mid-level discounts (20–35 percent) see if a lower level (e.g., changing a 35 percent discount to 25 percent, or changing 25 percent to 20 percent) wouldn't pull in just as many buyers. See Exhibit 16.7.

We offered consumers these discounts on five product categories, and used a brand name and an unknown brand for each product category (10 products total). As you can see

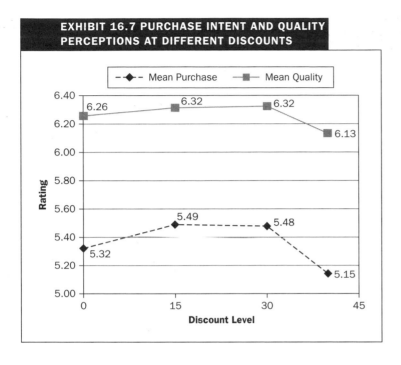

EXHIBIT 16.7 PURCHASE INTENT AND QUALITY PERCEPTIONS AT DIFFERENT DISCOUNTS

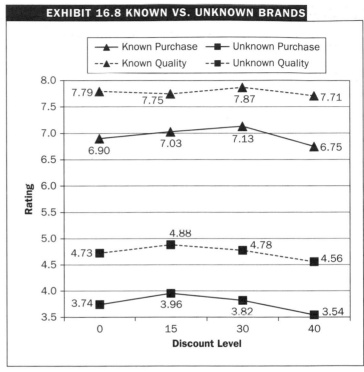

EXHIBIT 16.8 KNOWN VS. UNKNOWN BRANDS

from Exhibit 16.8, the known brand peaked at a 30 percent discount for both quality perception and purchase intention of consumers. The unknown brand peaked at a 15 percent discount level.

Note that the two upper (triangle) lines show a known brand—the top is the quality rating and just under it the purchase intention rating. The two lower (box) lines show the unknown brand.

There were also differences by product category. For example, purchase probability *decreased* from the

30 percent to the 40 percent discount for seven of the ten products:

- Both the known and unknown toothpaste
- Both the known and unknown yogurt
- Both the known and unknown tire
- The unknown brand only of vodka

For ABSOLUT vodka (the known brand), the discount level did not have a significant effect on purchase probability.

Concluding Thoughts on Pricing, and Especially on Testing Prices

You may believe because you hear little in the business press about price testing that not too many companies do it. But the lack of articles on the topic reflects how closed mouthed companies are about the topic—not how much of it is or isn't happening.

I found that out firsthand when I tried to launch a pricing forum on my PricingStrategyResources.com web site. It got twice as much traffic as the entire site had before, but I couldn't get anyone other than me to post pricing strategy, results, or ideas. Companies that understand pricing see that as a competitive advantage, and they seldom talk about it.

Non-marketers get very annoyed with us marketers, when our answer to most promotional ideas is: "I don't know. Let's test it!" But testing is truly the only way to know for sure which price will prove most profitable.

In this book, I've given you my insights and recommendations, based on more than two decades of pricing products and services, and testing prices. But whether they will work in your specific situation, neither you nor I can know for sure without you doing your own testing.

Appendix of Worksheets

These worksheets are here for your convenience, but they are much more valuable if you go to this book's companion web site (www.wiley.com/go/jensenprices). and use them as Excel spreadsheets. Many of the calculations are completed for you automatically in the Excel models.

The Competitor Pricing Worksheet

Chapter 3: Analyzing Your Competitors' Prices ©2013 PricingStrategyAssoc.com

SERVICE BUSINESS WORKSHEET

How to use this sheet: Pick the primary (in terms of quantity and profitability) services you offer and list in the first column. In the second "Add-Ons" column, list add-on services people can buy when they buy each primary service. Then list the names of your major competitors across the top row. Finally, find out (however you can) your competitors' prices for each and list them in the appropriate boxes. **FILL IN THE GREY BOXES!**

IN-A-RUSH TIPS: Don't skip this—it's one of the most critical steps. It will tell you what your targets EXPECT to pay, which is essential knowledge. However... **you can save time** by picking only your three or four main competitors and main services. But it will cost you some quality. For example, by looking at additional competitors you may find additional services they are offering that you might be able to profit from yourself!

(See the following pages for different types of business worksheets.)

Services and any add-ons to each service	Prices charged						
	Competitor1	Competitor2	Competitor3	Competitor4	Competitor5	Competitor6	Competitor7

List each of your primary services below, then (under "Add-ons") list separately anything you charge extra for when getting the listed service.

Service	Add-ons							
#1								

(Continued)

Service Business Worksheet *(Continued)*

Service	Add-ons	Prices charged						
		Competitor1	Competitor2	Competitor3	Competitor4	Competitor5	Competitor6	Competitor7
#2								
#3								
#4								
#5								
#6								

Chapter 3: Analyzing Your Competitors' Prices ©2013 PricingStrategyAssoc.com
PRODUCT BUSINESS WORKSHEET

How to use this sheet: Pick the primary (in terms of quantity and profitability) products you offer and list them down Column B. Also list (Column C) any add-on products people can buy when they buy each primary product. Then list the names of your major competitors across Row 8. Finally, find out (however you can) your competitors' prices for each and list them in the appropriate boxes. **FILL IN THE GREY BOXES!**

IN-A-RUSH TIPS: Don't skip this—it's one of the most critical steps. It will tell you what your targets EXPECT to pay, which is essential knowledge. However... you **can save time** by picking only your three or four main competitors and main products. But it will cost you some quality. For example, by looking at additional competitors you may find additional products they are offering that you might be able to profit from yourself!

(See the following pages for different types of business worksheets.)

Products and any add-ons to each product	Prices charged						
	Competitor1	Competitor2	Competitor3	Competitor4	Competitor5	Competitor6	Competitor7

List each of your primary products below, then (under "Add-ons") list separately anything you charge extra for that can be bought with the listed product.

	Product	Add-ons							
#1									
#2									
#3									
#4									

(Continued)

Product Business Worksheet *(Continued)*

| Product | Add-ons | Prices charged | | | | | | |
		Competitor1	Competitor2	Competitor3	Competitor4	Competitor5	Competitor6	Competitor7
#5								
#6								

Chapter 3: Analyzing Your Competitors' Prices ©2013 PricingStrategyAssoc.com
SPONSOR OPPORTUNITIES BUSINESS WORKSHEET

How to use this sheet: Pick the primary (in terms of quantity and profitability) sponsor opportunities you offer and list them down Column B. Also list (Column C) any add-on sponsor opportunities people can buy when they buy each primary sponsor opportunity. Then list the names of your major competitors across Row 8. Finally, find out (however you can) your competitors' prices for each and list them in the appropriate boxes. **FILL IN THE GREY BOXES!**

IN-A-RUSH TIPS: Don't skip this—it's one of the most critical steps. It will tell you what your targets EXPECT to pay, which is essential knowledge. However... **you can save time** by picking only your three or four main competitors and main sponsor opportunities. But it will cost you some quality. For example, by looking at additional competitors you may find additional sponsor opportunities they are offering that you might be able to profit from yourself!

(See the following pages for different types of business worksheets.)

	Prices charged						
Sponsor opportunities and any add-ons	Competitor1	Competitor2	Competitor3	Competitor4	Competitor5	Competitor6	Competitor7
List each of your primary sponsor opportunities below, then (under "Add-ons") list separately anything you charge extra for.							

Sponsor opportunity / **Add-ons**							
#1							
#2							
#3							

(Continued)

Sponsor Opportunities Business Worksheet (Continued)

Sponsor opportunity	Add-ons	Prices charged						
		Competitor1	Competitor2	Competitor3	Competitor4	Competitor5	Competitor6	Competitor7
#4								
#5								
#6								

The Buyer Benefits Worksheet

Chapter 6: Analyzing Buyer Benefits/Negatives Relative to Your Competitors ©2013 PricingStrategyAssoc.com

How to use this sheet: Don't list product attributes (e.g., 600 MB), but instead list the BENEFITS consumers get from them (e.g., faster speeds). **FILL IN THE GREY BOXES!**

IN-A-RUSH TIPS: Don't skip this—it's one of the most critical steps. It will tell you what your targets GET and what ANNOYS THEM in your marketplace. **You can save time** by picking only your three or four main competitors, but it will cost you some quality. For example, by looking at additional competitors you may find additional positives to add to your new product and/or negatives to remove.

Remove the examples in the grey boxes, then first list every benefit offered by your first competitor. Then list all additional benefits of your second. Then any additional of your third, etc. Finally list any new benefits from your offering. Checkmark which competitors offer each benefit.

	CONSUMER BENEFITS OFFERED						
	Competitor1	Competitor2	Competitor3	Competitor4	Competitor5	Competitor6	You
	[name]	[name]	[name]	[name]	[name]	[name]	Your Proposed Product
Overnight delivery	√		√		√	√	√
Highest quality					√	√	
Great warrantee allieviates risk	√	√		√			
Celebrity endorsement			√				
Payment can be spread over time							

(Continued)

The Buyer Benefits Worksheet (Continued)

First list every negative in your first competitor's product. Then list all additional negatives of your second. Then any additional of your third, etc. Finally list any new negatives from your offering. Checkmark which competitors have each negative. INCLUDE ALL NEGATIVES—even those all competitors have.

	CONSUMER NEGATIVES OFFERED						
	Competitor1	Competitor2	Competitor3	Competitor4	Competitor5	Competitor6	You
	[name]	[name]	[name]	[name]	[name]	[name]	Your Proposed Product
No overnight delivery offered	√	√	√	√	√	√	√
Poor quality					√	√	
Have to pay extra for a service agreement	√	√		√			
Unknown brand name			√				√

The Narrowing Your Price Range Worksheet

Chapter 7: Narrowing Your Price Range Worksheet ©2013 PricingStrategyAssoc.com

How to use this six-step worksheet: Review the material in Chapter 7, and in the Chapter 3 Worksheet. Be prepared to copy material from the Chapter 6 worksheet into this worksheet (to save time). **FILL IN THE GREY BOXES!**

IN-A-RUSH TIP: Don't skip this—it's one of the most critical steps.

STEP ONE:

Check which price position you're considering using:
Note: It's your price <u>relative to your competitors' prices</u>

	Penetration (low)	Premium/Prestige (high)	Competitive (in the middle)

STEP TWO:

Copy/paste the benefits and negatives below from your Chapter 6 Worksheet. Then copy/paste in ONLY the columns for your competitors who are closest to you in price position. Then add in the price for each from the Chapter 3 Worksheet.

Examples: If you choose Penetration pricing, pick only those competitors who have the 2–3 lowest prices. For Premium/Prestige pricing, copy the columns of the 2–3 highest-priced competitors. For Competitive pricing, copy in the columns of those competitors whose prices are in the middle.

YOUR COMPETITORS CLOSEST TO YOUR PRICE POSITION

Copy each competitor's name and check boxes from the Chapter 6 Worksheet

Price:	*Price:*	*Price:*	*Price:*	*Price:*
Competitor1	**Competitor2**	**Competitor3**	**Competitor4**	**You**
[name]	[name]	[name]	[name]	

BUYER BENEFITS

(Continued)

The Narrowing Your Price Range Worksheet *(Continued)*

BUYER BENEFITS

BUYER NEGATIVES

STEP THREE:

A. From the start of Step 2, list the LOWEST price of a competitor in this positioning:

B. From the start of Step 2, list the HIGHEST price of a competitor in this positioning:

The Narrowing Your Price Range Worksheet (Continued)

STEP FOUR:

A. Compare the **BENEFITS** of you and these specific competitors (lines 21–32, and check the box that most corresponds to how you stack up.

B. Compare the **NEGATIVES** of you and these specific competitors (lines 21–32, and check the box that most corresponds to how you stack up.

BETTER than most	About the SAME	WORSE than most

STEP FIVE:

Given how you stack up in benefits and negatives (Step 4), where in the price range from Step 3 should your price be?

Near the top	In the middle	Near the bottom

STEP SIX:

Return to Chapter 7 in your book to analyze your results here.

The Cost Analysis Worksheet

Chapter 8: Evaluating Your Costs ©2013 PricingStrategyAssoc.com

TOTAL OF ALL COSTS ON THE FOLLOWING THREE WORKSHEETS

IMPORTANT: *You don't have to enter anything on this sheet—it is done automatically from your entries on the other three worksheets in this file. (This worksheet especially works best if you go to the Web site and use the Excel version.)*

	Lowest Quantity You Might Sell	Lower-Middle Quantity	Higher-Middle Quantity	Highest Quantity You Might Sell
From Direct Costs worksheet				
Average MONTHLY UNIT sales estimate	0	0	0	0
Total MONTHLY direct per-unit costs	$0.00	$0.00	$0.00	$0.00
Total MONTHLY direct costs	**$0.00**	**$0.00**	**$0.00**	**$0.00**
From Fixed Overhead Costs worksheet				
Total MONTHLY overhead allocation	**$0**	**$0**	**$0**	**$0**
From Sunk-Costs Analysis worksheet				
Months sunk cost allocation must continue	0	0	0	0
Total MONTHLY sunk costs	**#DIV/0!**	**#DIV/0!**	**#DIV/0!**	**#DIV/0!**
TOTAL MONTHLY COSTS	#DIV/0!	#DIV/0!	#DIV/0!	#DIV/0!
TOTAL PER-UNIT COSTS (UNTIL sunk costs recovered)	**#DIV/0!**	**#DIV/0!**	**#DIV/0!**	**#DIV/0!**
TOTAL PER-UNIT COSTS (AFTER sunk costs recovered)	**#DIV/0!**	**#DIV/0!**	**#DIV/0!**	**#DIV/0!**

Chapter 8: Evaluating Your Costs ©2013 PricingStrategyAssoc.com

Direct Costs Worksheet

IMPORTANT:

Cells in grey REQUIRE your input.

Cells in dark grey only need your input IF your costs change based on the quantity you buy.

QUANTITY ANALYSIS

	Lowest	Lower-Middle	Higher-Middle	Highest
Quantity you estimate you will sell in an average MONTH				
Quantity your costs (below) based on:				

BULK COST ANALYSIS (Skip if you already have per-unit costs)

Production and Shipping

	Lowest	Lower-Middle	Higher-Middle	Highest
Materials or components you must purchase to include in this product/service you will be selling. <u>Price per quantity at the top of column.</u>				
Transportation costs, including mailing, shipping, and packaging <u>per quantity at top of column.</u>				
Total Costs for the column's quantity	$0.00	$0.00	$0.00	$0.00
Per-Unit Costs (Cell D20/D13) (Use in chart below.)	**#DIV/0!**	**#DIV/0!**	**#DIV/0!**	**#DIV/0!**

PER-UNIT COST ANALYSIS

Production and Shipping

	Lowest	Lower-Middle	Higher-Middle	Highest
Unit costs to you <u>per product</u> of any materials or components you must purchase to include in this product/service you will be selling				
Transportation costs, including mailing, shipping, and packaging <u>per product</u>				

Direct Selling Costs

	Lowest	Lower-Middle	Higher-Middle	Highest
Credit card fees. *(Multiply the % you will be charged times the highest price you are considering, then put that dollar amount here.)*				
Sales commissions (in $, not %) paid <u>per product sold</u>				
Other direct out-of-pocket costs that must be spent to sell <u>one</u> of these products. *(Do not include salaries/benefits.)*				
TOTAL PER-UNIT DIRECT COSTS	$0.00	$0.00	$0.00	$0.00

Chapter 8: Evaluating Your Costs ©2013 PricingStrategyAssoc.com

Overhead Costs Worksheet

IMPORTANT:

Enter your costs and % allocation for this product only in the grey cells.

FIXED OVERHEAD COSTS

(Annualize all these costs.)

	Actual annual $$	% of each allocated to this product/service	Allocated costs
Administrative			
Rent			$0
Electricity			$0
			$0
			$0
			$0
			$0
			$0
			$0
			$0
			$0
			$0
Sales-related			
Sales management salaries and benefits			$0
			$0
			$0
			$0
			$0
			$0
			$0
			$0
			$0
			$0
TOTAL ANNUAL OVERHEAD COSTS ALLOCATED TO YOUR PRODUCT/SERVICE			$0
AVERAGE PER MONTH			$0

Chapter 8: Evaluating Your Costs ©2013 PricingStrategyAssoc.com

Sunk Costs Worksheet

IMPORTANT:

Only the grey cells require your input.

Do NOT include any of the per-unit costs in these numbers.

SUNK-COST ANALYSIS—FOR THIS PRODUCT/SERVICE ONLY

Sunk Costs

Those expenses you've already incurred getting this new product/service
ready for market.

About-to-be-sunk Costs

Money you still have to spend getting this new product/service ready for
market.

PRE-LAUNCH TOTAL $0

Speed needed to recover sunk costs

How many months after launch do you have to recover your sunk costs?

(Some industries must do it in 3 months, others have 12 months or more.)

Enter the number of months you can spread the costs over:

SUNK COSTS/MONTH   #DIV/0!

Bibliography

Following are books and research articles that I have found interesting and/or informative on pricing. Those in academic journals will be rough reading for people not in academia, but if you skip to the "Results" and "Discussion" sections of the articles you can get all a practitioner needs from the articles. And the "Abstract" at the beginning of each article provides a quick skim to see if reading more is warranted for you.

Everything cited in this book can be found here but I've also listed more of my favorite books and articles, in case you find yourself as fascinated by pricing as I am and want to read more.

Abratt, R., and L. F. Pitt. (1985). "Pricing Practices in Two Industries." *Industrial Marketing Management, 14*(4), 301–306.

Adams, J. S. (1963). "Toward an Understanding of Inequity." *Journal of Abnormal and Social Psychology, 67*(4), 422–436.

Agrawal, D. (1996). "Effects of Brand Loyalty on Advertising and Trade Promotions: A Game Theoretic Analysis with Empirical Evidence." *Marketing Science, 15*(1), 86–108.

Alexander, C., and R. E. Goodhue. (2002). "The Pricing of Innovations: An Application to Specialized Corn Traits." *Agribusiness, 18*(3), 333–348.

Anonymous (2003). "Rate Increases." *Partner's Report, 2*(12), 7.

Ariely, D., G. Loewenstein, and D. Prelec. (2003). "'Coherent Arbitrariness': Stable Demand Curves without Stable Preferences." *The Quarterly Journal of Economics, 118*(1), 73–105.

Arnold, D. R., K. D. Hoffman, and J. McCormick. (1989). "Service Pricing: A Differentiation Premium Approach." *The Journal of Services Marketing, 3*(3), 25–32.

Atuahene-Gima, K. (1995). "An Exploratory Analysis of the Impact of Market Orientation on New Product Performance." *Journal of Product Innovation Management, 12*(4), 275–293.

Baker, W. E. (1999). "When Can Affective Conditioning and Mere Exposure Directly Influence Brand Choice?" *Journal of Advertising, 28*(4), 31–46.

Bettman, J. R. (1973). "Perceived Risk and its Components: A Model and Empirical Test." *Journal of Marketing Research, 10*(2), 184–190.

———. (1971). "The Structure of Consumer Choice Processes." *Journal of Marketing Research, 8*(4), 465–471.

Biswas, A., and E. A. Blair. (1991). "Contextual Effects of Reference Prices in Retail Advertisements." *Journal of Marketing, 55*(7), 1–12.

Biswas, A., C. Pullig, B. C. Krishnan, and S. Burton. (1999). "Consumer Evaluation of Reference Price Advertisements: Effects of Other Brands' Prices and Semantic Cues." *Journal of Public Policy & Marketing, 18*(1), 52–65.

Biswas, A., and D. L. Sherrell. (1993). "The Influence of Product Knowledge and Brand Name on Internal Price Standards and Confidence." *Psychology & Marketing, 10*(1), 31–46.

Blair, E.A., and E. L. Landon, Jr. (1981). "The Effects of Reference Prices in Retail Advertisements." *Journal of Marketing, 45*(Spring), 61–69.

Blattberg, R., T. Buesing, P. Peacock, and S. Sen. (1978). "Identifying the Deal Prone Segment." *Journal of Marketing Research, 15* (4), 369–377.

Blattberg, R., and S. K. Sen. (1976). "Market Segments and Stochastic Brand Choice Models." *Journal of Marketing Research, 13*(February), 33–45.

Blattberg, R. C., and K. J. Wisniewski. (1989). "Price-Induced Patterns of Competition." *Marketing Science, 8*(4), 291–310.

Brown, T. L., and J. W. Gentry. (1975). "Analysis of Risk and Risk-Reduction Strategies—a Multiple Product Case." *Journal of the Academy of Marketing Science, 3*(2), 148–160.

Butscher, S. A., and M. Laker. (2000). "Market-Driven Product Development: Using Target Costing to Optimize Products and Prices." *Marketing Management, 9*(2), 48–53.

Cannon, H. M., and F. W. Morgan. (1990). "A Strategic Pricing Framework." *Journal of Services Marketing, 4*(2), 19–30.

Cavallo, G. O., and M. L. Temares. (1969). "Brand Switching at the Point of Purchase." *Journal of Retailing, 45*(3), 27–36.

Chance, W. A., and N. D. French. (1972). "An Exploratory Investigation of Brand Switching." *Journal of Marketing Research, 9*(2), 226–269.

Chandrashekaran, R., and H. S. Jagpal. (1995). "Measuring Internal Reference Price: Some Preliminary Results." *Pricing Strategy & Practice, 3*(4), 28–34.

Chattopadhyay, A., and K. Basu. (1990). "Humor in Advertising: The Moderating Role of Prior Brand Evaluation." *Journal of Marketing Research, 27*(4), 466–476.

Compeau, L. D., and D. Grewal. (1998). "Comparative Price Advertising: An Integrative Review." *Journal of Public Policy & Marketing, 17*(2), 257–273.

Compeau, L. D., D. Grewal, and R. Chandrashekaran. (2002). "Comparative Price Advertising: Believe it or Not." *Journal of Consumer Affairs, 36*(2), 284–294.

Cooper, R. G. (1985). "Selecting Winning New Product Projects: Using the NewProd System." *Journal of Product Innovation Management, 2*(1), 34–44.

Coulter, K. S. (2001). "Odd-Ending Price Underestimation: An Experimental Examination of Left-to-Right Processing Effects." *Journal of Product & Brand Management, 10*(5), 276–292.

Cressman, G. S., Jr. (1999). "Commentary on: 'Industrial Pricing: Theory and Managerial Practice.'" *Marketing Science, 18*(3), 455–457.

Crowley, E., and J. Zajas. (1996). "Evidence Supporting the Importance of Brands in Marketing Computer Products." *Journal of Professional Services Marketing, 14*(2), 121–137.

Danaher, P. J. (2002). "Optimal Pricing of New Subscription Services: Analysis of a Market Experiment." *Marketing Science, 21*(2), 119–138.

Dawar, N., and P. Parker. (1994). "Marketing Universals: Consumers' Use of Brand Name, Price, Physical Appearance, and Retailer Reputation as Signals of Product Quality." *Journal of Marketing, 58*(2), 81–95.

de Chernatory, L., and S. Knox. (1992). "Brand Price Recall: The Implications for Pricing Research." *Marketing Intelligence & Planning, 10*(9), 17–20.

Della Bitta, A. J., K. B. Monroe, and J. M. McGinnis. (1981). "Consumers' Perception of Comparative Price Advertisements." *Journal of Marketing Research, 18*(4), 416–427.

Desmet, P. (1999). "Asking for Less to Obtain More." *Journal of Interactive Marketing, 13*(3), 55–65.

Dhar, R., and I. Simonson. (1992). "The Effect of the Focus of Comparison on Consumer Preferences." *Journal of Marketing Research, 29*(4), 430–440.

Diller, H., and A. Brielmaier. (1995). "The Impact of Rounding-up Odd Prices: Results of a Field Experiment in German Drugstores." *Pricing Strategy & Practice, 3*(4), 4–13.

Dodds, W. B., K. B. Monroe, and D. Grewal. (1991). "Effects of Price, Brand and Store Information on Buyers' Product Evaluations." *Journal of Marketing Research, 28*(3), 307–319.

Dodson, J. A., A. M. Tybout, and B. Sternthal. (1978). "Impact of Deals and Deal Retraction on Brand Switching." *Journal of Marketing Research, 15*(1), 72–81.

Dolan, R. J., and H. Simon. (1996). *Power Pricing* (pp. 4–5). New York: The Free Press.

Dowling, G. R. (1986). "Perceived Risk: The Concept and its Measurement." *Psychology & Marketing, 3*(3), 193–210.

Dowling, G. R., and R. Staelin. (1994). "A Model of Perceived Risk and Intended Risk-Handling Activity." *Journal of Consumer Research 21*(1), 119–134.

Drozdenko, R., and M. Jensen. (2005). "Risk and Acceptable Maximum Discount Levels." *Journal of Product & Brand Management, 14*(4), 264–270.

Drozdenko, R., and M. Jensen. (2003). "Factors Influencing Brand Switching: Age, Sex and Brand Loyalty Groupings." *Proceedings of Northeast Business & Economics Association, Montclair State University, 30, 18–21.*

Erdem, T., G. Mayhew, and B. Sun. (2001). "Understanding Reference-Price Shoppers: A Within- and Cross-Category Analysis." *Journal of Marketing Research, 38*(4), 445–457.

Erickson, G. M., and J. K. Johansson. (1985). "The Role of Price in Multi-Attribute Product Evaluations." *Journal of Consumer Research, 12*(2), 195–199.

Estelami, H. (2009). *Marketing Turnarounds.* Indianapolis, Ind.: Dog Ear Publishing.

Festinger, L. (1957). *A Theory of Cognitive Dissonance.* Sanford, Calif.: Stanford University Press.

Fouilhe, P. (1970). "The Subjective Evaluation of Price: Methodological Aspects," in B. Taylor, and G. Wills (Eds.), *Pricing Strategy* (pp. 89–97). Princeton, N.J.: Brandon/Systems Press.

Fraccastoro, K., S. Burton, and A. Biswas. (1993). "Effective Use of Advertisements Promoting Sale Prices." *Journal of Consumer Marketing, 10*(1), 61–70.

Frank, R. E., W. F. Massy, and T. M. Lodahl. (1969). "Purchasing Behavior and Personal Attributes." *Journal of Advertising Research, 9*(4), 15–24.

Frankenberger, K. D., and R. Liu. (1994). "Does Consumer Knowledge Affect Consumer Responses to Advertised Reference Price Claims?" *Psychology & Marketing, 11*(3), 235–251.

Gabor, A., and C. W. J. Granger. (1966). "Price as an Indicator of Quality: Report on an Enquiry." *Economica, 33*(129), 43–70.

Gardner, D. M. (1971). "Is There a Generalized Price-Quality Relationship?" *Journal of Marketing Research, 8*(2), 241–243.

Gliner, J. A., and G. A. Morgan. (2000). *Research Methods in Applied Settings*. Mahwah, NJ: Lawrence Erlbaum Associates.

Gonul, F. F., P. T. L. Leszczyc, and T. Sugawara. (1996). "Joint Estimates of Purchase Timing and Brand Switch Tendency: Results from a Scanner Panel Data Set of Frequently Purchased Products." *Canadian Journal of Economics, 29*(April), S501–S526.

Grewal, D., J. Gotlieb, and H. Marmorstein. (1994). "The Moderating Effects of Message Framing and Source Credibility on the Price-Perceived Risk Relationship." *Journal of Consumer Research, 21*(1), 145–153.

Grewal, D., K. B. Monroe, and R. Krishnan. (1998). "The Effects of Price-Comparison Advertising on Buyers' Perceptions of Acquisition Value, Transaction Value, and Behavioral Intentions." *Journal of Marketing, 62*(4), 46–59.

Gruber, M. (2004). "Marketing in New Ventures: Theory and Empirical Evidence." *Schmalenbach Business Review, 56*(2), 164–199.

Gupta, S., and L. G. Cooper. (1992). "The Discounting of Discounts and Promotion Thresholds." *Journal of Consumer Research, 19*(3), 401–412.

Han, S., S. Gupta, and D. R. Lehmann. (2001). "Consumer Price Sensitivity and Price Thresholds." *Journal of Retailing, 77*, 435–456.

Hanlon, D., and D. Luery. (2002). "The Role of Pricing Research in Assessing the Commercial Potential of New Drugs in Development." *International Journal of Market Research, 44*(4), 423–447.

Hauser, J. R. (1988). "Competitive Price and Positioning Strategies." *Marketing Science, 7*(1), 76–91.

Hauser, J. R., and S. P. Gaskin. (1984). "Application of the 'Defender' Consumer Model." *Marketing Science, 3*(4), 327–351.

Heider, F. (1958). *The Psychology of Interpersonal Relations*. New York: John Wiley & Sons.

Helgeson, J. G., and S. E. Beatty. (1987). "Price Expectation and Price Recall Error: An Empirical Study." *Journal of Consumer Research, 14*(3), 379–386.

Helson, H. (1964). *Adaptation Level Theory*. New York: Harper & Row Publishers.

Henard, D. H., and D. M. Szymanski. (2001). "Why Some New Products Are More Successful than Others." *Journal of Marketing Research, 38*(3), 362–375.

Hoeffler, S., and K. L. Keller. (2003). "The Marketing Advantages of Strong Brands." *Journal of Brand Management, 10*(6), 421–445.

Hoffman, K. D., and D. R. Arnold. (1989). "Professional Services Pricing: An Extended Cost-Oriented Approach." *Journal of Professional Services Marketing, 5*(1), 29–40.

Hogan, J. (2005). "Driving Growth with New Products: How to Avoid New Product Pricing Traps." *The Pricing Advisor, 1*(2).

Holden, S. J. S., and M. Vanhuele. (1999). "Know the Name, Forget the Exposure: Brand Familiarity versus Memory of Exposure Context." *Psychology & Marketing, 16*(6), 479–496.

Huppertz, J. W., S. J. Arenson, and R. H. Evans. (1978). "An Application of Equity Theory to Buyer-Seller Exchange Situations." *Journal of Marketing Research, 15*(2), 250–260.

Ingenbleek, P., M. Debruyne, R. T. Frambach, and T. M. M. Verhallen. (2003). "Successful New Product Pricing Practices: A Contingency Approach." *Marketing Letters, 14*(4), 289–305.

Inman, J. J., and M. Zeelenberg. (2002). "Regret in Repeat Purchase versus Switching Decisions: The Attenuating Role of Decision Justifiability." *Journal of Consumer Research, 29*(1), 116–128.

Jacoby, J., J. Olson, and R. Haddock. (1971). "Price, Brand Name and Product Composition Characteristics as Determinants of Perceived Quality." *Journal of Applied Psychology, 55*(6), 570–579.

Janiszewski, C., and M. Cunha, Jr. (2004). "The Influence of Price Discount Framing on the Evaluation of a Product Bundle." *Journal of Consumer Research, 30*(4), 534–546.

Janiszewski, C., and D. R. Lichtenstein. (1999). "A Range Theory Account of Price Perception." *Journal of Consumer Research, 25*(4), 353–368.

Jensen, M. (2005). "New Product Pricing Model and Decision Tree." Unpublished manuscript.

Jensen, M., and R. Drozdenko. (2006). "Risk and Competitive Price Positioning." Unpublished raw data.

———. (2004). "The Effects of Discount Levels on Purchase Intention and Quality Perception," in N. Delener (Chair), *Marketing—Diverse Issues.* Symposium conducted at the 31st Annual Northeast Business & Economics Assn., Yeshiva University, New York City.

Jensen, T., J. Kees, S. Burton, and F. L. Turnipseed. (2003). "Advertised Reference Prices in an Internet Environment: Effects on Consumer Price Perceptions and Channel Search Intentions." *Journal of Interactive Marketing, 17*(2), 20–33.

Johnson, E. J., and J. E. Russo. (1984). "Product Familiarity and Learning New Information." *Journal of Consumer Research, 11*(1), 542–550.

Kahneman, D., and D. T. Miller. (1986). "Norm Theory: Comparing Reality to its Alternatives." *Psychological Review, 93*(2), 136–153.

Kahneman, D., and A. Tversky. (1979). "Prospect Theory: An Analysis of Decision under Risk." *Econometrica, 47*(2), 263–291.

Kalyanaram, G., and J. D. C. Little. (1994). "An Empirical Analysis of Latitude of Price Acceptance in Consumer Package Goods." *Journal of Consumer Research, 21*(3), 408–418.

Kamen, J., and R. J. Toman. (1970). "Psychophysics of Prices." *Journal of Marketing Research, 7*(1), 27–35.

Kamins, M. A., X. Dreze, and V. S. Folkes. (2004). "Effects of Seller-Supplied Prices on Buyers' Product Evaluations: Reference Prices in an Internet Auction Context." *Journal of Consumer Research, 30*(3), 622–628.

Kara, A., E. Kaynak, and O. Kucukemiroglu. (1994). "Credit Card Development Strategies for the Youth Market: The Use of Conjoint Analysis." *The International Journal of Bank Marketing, 12*(6), 30–36.

Keller, K. L. (1993). "Conceptualizing, Measuring, and Managing Customer-Based Brand Equity." *Journal of Marketing, 57*(1), 1–22.

Kerin, R. A., S. W. Hartley, E. N. Berkowitz, and W. Rudelius. (2006). *Marketing.* New York: McGraw-Hill Irwin.

Kim, W. C. and Mauborgne, R. (2005). *Blue Ocean Strategy.* Boston: Harvard Business School Press.

Kohli, R., and V. Mahajan. (1991). "A Reservation-Price Model for Optimal Pricing of Multiattribute Products in Conjoint Analysis." *Journal of Marketing Research, 28*(3), 347–354.

Kotler, P., and K. L. Keller. (2005). *Marketing Management.* Upper Saddle River, NJ: Prentice Hall.

Krider, R. E., and S. Han. (2004). "Promotion Thresholds: Price Change Insensitivity or Risk Hurdle?" *Journal of Administrative Sciences, 21*(3), 255–271.

Krishna, A., M. Wagner, C. Yoon, and R. Adaval. (2006). "Effects of Extreme-Priced Products on Consumer Reservation Prices." *Journal of Consumer Psychology, 16*(2), 176–190.

Krishnamurthi, L., T. Mazumdar, and S. P. Raj. (1992). "Asymmetric Response to Price in Consumer Brand Choice and Purchase Quantity Decisions." *Journal of Consumer Research, 19*(3), 387–400.

Lambert, Z. V. (1972). "Price and Choice Behavior." *Journal of Marketing Research, 9*(1), 35–40.

Lawrence, R. J. (1969). "Patterns of Buyer Behavior: Time for a New Approach?" *Journal of Marketing Research, 6*(2), 137–144.

Le Bon, J., and D. Merunka. (1999). "Explaining and Managing Salespeople's Effort Towards Competitive Intelligence: Evidences from the C.I.A. Salesperson Scale." *Proceedings of the American Marketing Association, USA, 10*, 56–57.

Lee, Y., and G. C. O'Connor. (2003). "New Product Launch Strategy for Network Effects Products." *Academy of Marketing Science Journal, 31*(3), 241–255.

Lehmann, D. R., and Y. Pan. (1994). "Context Effects, New Brand Entry, and Consideration Sets." *Journal of Marketing Research, 31*(3), 364–374.

Licata, J. W., A. Biswas, and B. C. Krishnan. (1998). "Ambiguity and Exaggeration in Price Promotion: Perceptions of the Elder and Nonelder Consumer." *Journal of Consumer Affairs, 32*(1), 56–81.

Lichtenstein, D. R., S. Burton, and B. S. O'Hara. (1989). "Marketplace Attributions and Consumer Evaluations of Discount Claims." *Psychology & Marketing, 6*(3), 163–180.

Lindsey-Mullikin, J. (2003). "Beyond Reference Price: Understanding Consumers' Encounters with Unexpected Prices." *The Journal of Product and Brand Management, 12*(2/3), 140–153.

Lowengart, O., S. Mizrahi, and R. Yosef. (2003). "Effect of Consumer Characteristics on Optimal Reference Price." *Journal of Revenue and Pricing Management, 2*(3), 201–215.

Lu, Z. J., and W. S. Comanor. (1998). "Strategic Pricing of New Pharmaceuticals." *The Review of Economics and Statistics, 80*(1), 108.

Madan, V., and R. Suri. (2001). "Quality Perception and Monetary Sacrifice: A Comparative Analysis of Discount and Fixed Prices." *Journal of Product & Brand Management, 10*(3), 170–82.

Marshall, R., and S. B. Leng. (2002). "Price Threshold and Discount Saturation Point in Singapore." *Journal of Product & Brand Management, 11*(3), 147–159.

Matanovich, T., G. L. Lilien, and A. Rangaswamy. (1999). "Engineering the Price-Value Relationship." *Marketing Management, 8*(1), 48–53.

Mathur, L. K., I. Mathur, and N. Rangan. (1997). "The Wealth Effects Associated with a Celebrity Endorser: The Michael Jordan Phenomenon." *Journal of Advertising Research, 37*(3), 67–73.

Mayhew, G. E. and R. S. Winer. (1992). "An Empirical Analysis of Internal and External Reference Prices Using Scanner Data." *Journal of Consumer Research, 19*(1), 62–70.

Maxwell, S. (2008). *The Price Is Wrong: Understanding What Makes a Price Seem Fair and the True Cost of Unfair Pricing.* Hoboken, NJ: John Wiley & Sons.

Mazumdar, R., and P. Papatla. (2000). "An Investigation of Reference Price Segments." *Journal of Marketing Research, 37*(2), 246–258.

McAlister, L. (1986). *The Impact of Price Promotions on a Brand's Market Share, Sales Pattern, and Profitability.* Cambridge, Mass.: Marketing Science Institute.

McConnell, J. D. (1980). "Comment on 'A Major Price-Perceived Quality Study Reexamined.'" *Journal of Marketing Research, 17*(May), 263–264.

———. (1968). "The Price-Quality Relationship in an Experimental Setting." *Journal of Marketing Research, 5*(3), 300–303.

Mobley, M. F., W. O. Bearden, and J. E. Teel. (1988). "An Investigation of Individual Responses to Tensile Price Claims." *Journal of Consumer Research, 15*(9), 273–279.

Monger, J. E., and R. A. Feinberg. (1997). "Mode of Payment and Formation of Reference Prices." *Pricing Strategy & Practice, 5*(4), 142–148.

Monroe, K. B. (1990). *Pricing: Making Profitable Decisions.* New York: McGraw-Hill Publishing.

———. (1973). "Buyers' Subjective Perceptions of Price." *Journal of Marketing Research, 10*(1), 70–80.

———. (1971a). "Measuring Price Thresholds by Psychophysics and Latitudes of Acceptance." *Journal of Marketing Research, 8*(4), 460–464.

———. (1971b). "Psychophysics of Prices: A Reappraisal." *Journal of Marketing Research, 8*(2), 248–251.

Monroe, K. B., and T. Mazumdar. (1988). "Pricing-Decision Models: Recent Developments and Research Opportunities," in Devinney, T. M. (ed.), *Issues in Pricing, Theory and Research.* Lexington, MA: Lexington Books.

Moore, D. J., and R. W. Olshavsky. (1989). "Brand Choice and Deep Price Discounts." *Psychology & Marketing, 6*(3), 181–196.

Muthukrishnam, A. V. (1995). "Decision Ambiguity and Incumbent Brand Advantage." *Journal of Consumer Research, 22*(1), 98–109.

Myers, M. B., S. T. Cavusgil, and A. Diamantopoulos. (2002). "Antecedents and Actions of Export Pricing Strategy." *European Journal of Marketing, 36*(1/2), 159–188.

Nagle, T. T., and R. K. Holden. (2002). *The Strategy and Tactics of Pricing* (5th ed.). Upper Saddle River, NJ: Prentice Hall.

Naipaul, S., and H. G. Parsa. (2001). Menu price endings that communicate value and quality. *Cornell Hotel and Restaurant Administration Quarterly, 42*(1), 26–37.

Neuhaus, C. F., and J. R. Taylor. (1972). "Variables Affecting Sales of Family-Branded Products." *Journal of Marketing Research, 9*(4), 419.

Niedrich, R. W., S. Sharma, S., and D. H. Wedell. (2001). "Reference Price and Price Perceptions: A Comparison of Alternative Models." *Journal of Consumer Research, 28*(3), 339–354.

Noble, P. M., and T. S. Gruca. (1999). "Industrial Pricing: Theory and Managerial Practice." *Marketing Science, 18*(3), 135–154.

Ofir, C. (2004). "Reexamining Latitude of Price Acceptability and Price Thresholds: Predicting Basic Consumer Reaction to Price." *Journal of Consumer Research, 30*(4), 612–621.

Olander, F. (1970). "The Influence of Price on the Consumer's Evaluation of Products and Purchases," in B. Taylor, and G. Wills (Eds.), *Pricing Strategy* (pp. 50–69). Princeton, NJ: Brandon/Systems Press.

Ong, B. S., and T. D. Jensen. (1996). "Reference Price-Quality Claims Effects on Purchase Evaluations." *Pricing Strategy & Practice, 4*(4), 25–34.

Oxenfeldt, A. R. (1973). "A Decision-Making Structure for Price Decisions." *Journal of Marketing, 37*(1), 48–53.

Park, C. S., and V. Srinivasan. (1994). "A Survey-Based Method for Measuring and Understanding Brand Equity and its Extendibility." *Journal of Marketing Research, 31*(2), 271–288.

Peter, J. P., and L. X. Tarpey, Sr. (1975). "A Comparative Analysis of Three Consumer Decision Strategies." *Journal of Consumer Research, 2*(1), 29–36.

Peterson, R. A., and W. Wilson. (1985). "Perceived Risk and Price-Reliance Schema as Price-Perceived-Quality Mediators," in Jacoby, J., and J. C. Olson (Eds.), *Perceived Quality: How Consumers View Stores and Merchandise* (pp. 248–268). Lexington, MA: Lexington Books.

Petroshius, S. M., and K. B. Monroe. (1987). "Effect of Product-Line Pricing Characteristics on Product Evaluations." *Journal of Consumer Research, 13*(4), 511–519.

Purducci, A. (1965). "Category Judgment: A Range-Frequency Model." *Psychological Review, 72*(6), 407–418.

Puto, C. P. (1987). "The Framing of Buying Decisions." *Journal of Consumer Research, 14*(3), 301–315.

Rafi, M. (2005). *The Art of Pricing.* New York: Crown Business.

Raj, A., and C. Stoner. (1996). "The Effect of Perceived Service Quality and Name Familiarity on the Service

Selection Decision." *The Journal of Services Marketing, 10*(1), 22–35.

Rajendran, K. N., and G. J. Tellis. (1994). "Contextual and Temporal Components of Reference Price." *Journal of Marketing, 58*(1), 22–34.

Raju, J. S., V. Srinivasan, et al. (1990). "The Effects of Brand Loyalty on Competitive Price Promotion Strategies." *Management Science, 36*(3), 276.

Rao, V. R. (1984). "Pricing Research in Marketing: The State of the Art." *Journal of Business, 57*(1), 39–60.

Rao, V. (1971). "Salience of Price in the Perception of Product Quality: A Multidimensional Measurement Approach," in American Marketing Association, *Combined Proceedings, Spring & Fall Conferences* (pp. 571–577). Chicago, Ill.: American Marketing Association.

Rao, A. R., and W. A. Sieben. (1992). "The Effect of Prior Knowledge on Price Acceptability and the Type of Information Examined." *Journal of Consumer Research, 19*(2), 256–270.

Ries, A., and J. Trout. (1972). *Positioning: The Battle for Your Mind.* New York: McGraw-Hill.

Sapede, C., and I. Girod. (2002). "Willingness of Adults in Europe to Pay for a New Vaccine: The Application of Discrete Choice-Based Conjoint Analysis." *International Journal of Market Research, 44*(4), 463–491.

Saunders, J., and F. Guoqun. (1996). "Dual Branding: How Corporate Names Add Value." *Marketing Intelligence & Planning, 14*(7), 29–35.

Scherer, R. M. (1980). *Industrial Market Structure and Economic Performance.* Chicago: Rand McNally.

Schiffman, L. G., and L. L. Kanuk. (2004). *Consumer Behavior.* Upper Saddle River, NJ: Pearson Prentice Hall.

Shapiro, B. (1977). *Deere & Company: Industrial Equipment Operations,* Case 577–112, Boston, MA: Harvard Business School.

Shapiro, B. P. (1973). "Price Reliance: Existence and Sources." *Journal of Marketing Research, 10*(3), 286–294.

Sherif, C., and C. E. Hovland. (1964). *Social Judgment.* New Haven, CT: Yale University Press.

Silverstein, M. J., and N. Fiske. (2003, 2005). *Trading Up.* New York: Penguin Group.

Simonson, I., J. Huber, and J. Payne. (1988). "The Relationship between Prior Brand Knowledge and Information Acquisition Order." *Journal of Consumer Research, 14*(4), 566–578.

Sivakumar, K., and S. P. Raj. (1997). "Quality Tier Competition: How Price Change Influences Brand Choice and Category Choice." *Journal of Marketing, 16*(3), 71–84.

Smith, S. A. (1986). "New Product Pricing in Quality Sensitive Markets." *Marketing Science, 5*(1), 70–87.

Smith, E., and C. Broome. (1966). "A Laboratory Experiment for Establishing Indifference Prices between Brands of Consumer Products," in American Marketing Association, *Fall Conference Proceedings* (pp. 511–519). Chicago: American Marketing Association.

———. (1966). "Experimental Determination of the Effect of Price and Market-Standing Information on Consumers' Brand Preferences," in American Marketing Association, *Fall Conference Proceedings* (pp. 520–531). Chicago: American Marketing Association.

Solomon, M. R., G. W. Marshall, and E. W. Stuart. (2012). *Marketing: Real People Real Choices.* Upper Saddle River, NJ: Prentice Hall.

Stafford, J., and B. Enis. (1969). "The Price-Quality Relationship: An Extension." *Journal of Marketing Research, 6*(4), 456–458.

Stiving, M., and R. S. Winer. (1997). "An Empirical Analysis of Price Endings with Scanner Data." *Journal of Consumer Research, 24*(1), 57–67.

Suri, R., R. Manchanda, and C. Kohli. (2000). "Brand Evaluations: A Comparison of Fixed Price and Discounted Price Offers." *Journal of Product and Brand Management, 9*(3), 193–204.

Suter, T. A., and S. Burton. (1996). "Believability and Consumer Perceptions of Implausible Reference Prices in Retail Advertisements." *Psychology & Marketing, 13*(1), 37–54.

Taylor, J. W. (1974). "The Role of Risk in Consumer Behavior." *Journal of Marketing, 39*(April), 54–60.

Tellis, G. J. (1988). "Advertising Exposure, Loyalty, and Brand Purchase: A Two-Stage Model of Choice." *Journal of Marketing Research, 25*(2), 134–144.

———. (1988). "The Price Elasticity of Selective Demand: A Meta-Analysis of Econometric Models of Sales." *Journal of Marketing Research, 25*(4), 331–341.

Thaler, R. H. (1985). "Mental Accounting and Consumer Choice." *Marketing Science, 4*(3), 199–214.

Thomas, M., and V. Morwitz. (2005). "Penny Wise and Pound Foolish: The Left-Digit Effect in Price Cognition." *Journal of Consumer Research, 32*(1), 54–64.

"Tips to Jump-Start New-Product Marketing." (2006). *AMA's Marketing Thought Leaders Newsletter* (April 12), 1–2.

Tull, D., R. A. Boring, and M. H. Gonsior. (1964). "A Note on the Relationship of Price and Imputed Quality." *Journal of Business, 37*(2), 186–91.

Tversky, A., and D. Kahneman. (1974). "Judgment under Uncertainty: Heuristics and Biases." *Science, 185*(Sept.) 1124–1131.

Tzokas, N., S. Hart, P. Argouslidis, and M. Saren. (2000). "Industrial Export Pricing Practices in the United Kingdom." *Industrial Marketing Management, 29*(May), 191–210.

Udell, G. G., and T. A. Potter. (1989). "Pricing New Technology." *Research Technology Management, 32*(4), 14–18.

Urban, G. L. (1980). *Design and Marketing of New Products.* Englewood Cliffs, N.J.: Prentice-Hall.

Urbany, J. E., W. O. Bearden, A. Kaicker, and M. Smith-de Borrero. (1997). "Transaction Utility Effects When Quality Is Uncertain." *Journal of the Academy of Marketing Science, 25*(1), 45–55.

Urbany, J. E., W. O. Bearden, and D. C. Weilbaker. (1988). "The Effect of Plausible and Exaggerated Reference Prices on Consumer Perceptions and Price Search." *Journal of Consumer Research, 15*(June), 95–110.

Urbany, J. E., and P. R. Dickson. (1991). "Consumer Normal Price Estimation: Market versus Personal Standards." *Journal of Consumer Research, 18*(1), 45–51.

Volkmann, J. (1951). "Scales of Judgment and Their Implications for Social Psychology," in J. H. Rohrer, and M. Sherif (Ed.), *Social Psychology at the Crossroads* (pp. 273–294). New York: Harper.

Wansink, B., R. J. Kent, and S. J. Hoch. (1998). "An Anchoring and Adjustment Model of Purchase Quantity Decisions." *Journal of Marketing Research, 35*(1), 71–81.

Weber, J. E., and R. W. Hansen. (1972). "The Majority Effect and Brand Choice." *Journal of Marketing Research, 9*(August), 320–23.

Weerahandi, S., and S. Moitra. (1995). "Using Survey Data to Predict Adoption and Switching for Services." *Journal of Marketing Research, 32*(1), 85–96.

Winer, R. S. (1986). "A Reference Price Model of Brand Choice for Frequently Purchased Products." *Journal of Consumer Research, 13*(2), 250–256.

———. (1985). "A Price Vector Model of Demand for Consumer Durables: Preliminary Developments." *Marketing Science, 4*(1), 74–90.

Zaichkowsky, J. L. (1985). "Measuring the Involvement Construct." *Journal of Consumer Research, 12*(3), 341–335.

Zais, H. W. (1977). "Economic Modeling: An Aid to the Pricing of Information Services." *Journal of the American Society for Information Science, 28*(2), 89–95.

Zubey, M. L., W. Wagner, and J. R. Otto. (2002). "A Conjoint Analysis of Voice over IP Attributes." *Internet Research, 12*(1), 7–15.

About the Author

Marlene Jensen is on a mission to help entrepreneurs launch successful companies (pricing is usually a critical problem for them) and to help established companies price more profitably.

- She's a pricing and marketing consultant (Pricing Strategy Associates).

- She has a doctorate in marketing and wrote her dissertation on pricing new products.

- She specializes in helping small and new businesses, although she has worked or consulted for some very big companies, including AARP, CBS, ABC, *Playboy*, and Food Network.

- She's taught pricing, marketing and entrepreneurship at a number of universities, including New York University and the Ancell School of Business at Western Connecticut State University. She's now an associate professor of marketing at Lock Haven University.

- Her research studies on pricing have been presented at prestigious academic conferences in New York City, Philadelphia, Orlando, Las Vegas, Detroit, Syracuse, and Newport, Rhode Island.

- Her pricing research has been published in a number of academic journals, including the *Journal of Product & Brand Management,* the *International Journal of Revenue Management,* and the *International Journal of Business, Marketing, and Decision Sciences.*

- She's the author of four books on pricing (this one, plus *Pricing Psychology Report, 46 Ways to Raise Prices,* and *The Tao of Pricing*). Each of these books is targeted to entrepreneurs and marketing practitioners, not to academia.

Pricing web sites owned and operated by the author are:

- PricingStrategyAssoc.com

- PricingStrategyResources.com

- PricingPsychology.com

- RaiseYourPrices.com

- TaoOfPricing.com

About the Companion Web Site

Visit this book's companion web site at www.wiley .com/go/jensenprices (password: PriceSetting Jensen). There you will find various tools to use alongside the chapters in this book, including four Excel worksheets as follows:

- Chapter 3: The Competitor Pricing Worksheet
- Chapter 6: The Buyer Benefits Worksheet

- Chapter 7: The Narrowing Your Price Range Worksheet
- Chapter 8: The Cost Analysis Worksheet

You can use these four worksheets as directed within the book to help you in your pricing strategy.

Index